THE RUDIMENTS OF CRITICISM

BY

E. A. GREENING LAMBORN
HEAD MASTER OF THE EAST OXFORD SCHOOL

SECOND EDITION

OXFORD
AT THE CLARENDON PRESS

OXFORD
UNIVERSITY PRESS
LONDON : AMEN HOUSE, E.C. 4
EDINBURGH GLASGOW LEIPZIG
COPENHAGEN NEW YORK TORONTO
MELBOURNE CAPETOWN BOMBAY
CALCUTTA MADRAS SHANGHAI
HUMPHREY MILFORD
PUBLISHER TO THE
UNIVERSITY

Impression of 1928
First edition, 1916
Second edition, 1925

PREFACE

'I COULD wish that there were authors of this kind, who, besides the mechanical rules, which a man of very little taste may discourse upon, would enter into the very spirit and soul of fine writing and show us the several sources of that pleasure which rises in the mind upon the perusal of a noble work . . . which few of the critics besides Longinus have considered.'

We cannot complain that Addison's wish has not been amply fulfilled in the last century and in our own day by the critics both of England and France. Yet I believe it is still true that no one since Longinus has given us, point by point, in a small compass and in a simple style, a general introduction to the meaning and scope of criticism. There are numerous and admirable books on particular poets and poems and periods, but I do not know of any modern 'Poetics', a general study of poetic form, on the model of the treatise of Longinus 'On the Sublime', with illustrations from our own poets. Moreover, all the critical studies that I know are for the advanced student, they preach to the converted, to those who have already learned to love poetry. For a long time I have been looking for a simply-written introduction to the study of poetry such as might be put into the hands of young students to show them what to look for and to prevent them falling at the outset into the fatal error of reading poetry for the substance and not the form of its matter: this is the error of the annotated editions which are the common substitute for the kind of book I mean, and not one student in a hundred survives their vicious influence. If such a book exists my excuse for the present essay is gone. I began it with no thought of publication, but simply with the idea of setting down, for the use of my staff and of the young teachers whose practice I supervise, some record of methods I had found useful in my own lessons, and some suggestions and conclusions drawn from my experience as a teacher and a student of literature. But I have been led to suppose that the notes may be helpful in other schools and training colleges; and I should like to cherish a hope that they might be the means of leading some, whom the schools have failed to persuade, to the study and appreciation of poetry.

CONTENTS

None of us yet know, for to none has it yet been revealed in early youth, what fairy palaces we may build for ourselves of beautiful thoughts - proof against all adversity.—RUSKIN.

INTRODUCTION

> Thy mind
> Shall be a mansion for all lovely thoughts,
> Thy memory be as a dwelling-place
> For all sweet sounds and harmonies.

I BELIEVE that 'why?' is always a more important question than 'how?' for Englishmen especially and for teachers in particular. We are so fond of action that we do not care to think of aims; we are so eager for results that we seldom pause to consider if they are really worthy of our efforts. So long as something is attempted, something done, we do not often ask whether that thing is the best which could occupy us in the circumstances. And when we do we are apt to be content with the answers of tradition. This may be a source of strength as well as of weakness in a nation; but I agree with those[1] who have declared it to be the origin of much mistaken teaching in the elementary schools.

So although the essay is concerned mainly with methods, I will begin by stating the end at which all art teaching should aim: it is, in a word, Appreciation, which is a form of Appraising, which, shortly, is Praise; it is to learn the true value of a work of art that we may admire and love it.

Though in the material sense of utility it is true that 'all art is useless', yet in a deeper and far more real sense 'studies that serve for delight', like poetry, are the very end for which utilitarian science and skill exist; we learn and labour to provide material things in order

[1] e. g. Mr. E. G. A. Holmes in 'What Is and What Might Be'.

that we may enjoy spiritual things. But that poetry is not a means of supplying useful information or of training the memory—except to learn more poetry—or improving the morals, or providing sage axioms or grammatical examples, or serving any practical purpose, let us with joy admit and declare. It is the charm and the glory of poetry that its high and single purpose is 'to make glad the heart of man'.

But, like all the fine arts, it will only yield its full delight to the trained seeker, the critic—in the true meaning of that much-abused word.

Those who think of the difficulties and drudgery of the old days, when so many lines 'with knowledge of meanings and allusions' had to be taught each year; of the annotated editions with three pages of notes to two of poetry; and of the difficulty in making children remember that the Mincius is a tributary of the Po, that a prism—'prisms in every carven glass'—is a solid figure whose sides are parallelograms, the ends, whatever their shapes, being equal and parallel, that *samite* is Greek *hexamiton* and German *sammet* which is English velvet, that Idylls, Eclogues, and Bucolics are, more or less, names for the same thing—I am quoting actual notes,[1] not drawing on memory or imagination—may fear that real criticism is too difficult a matter for children. If that were indeed so we ought to abolish poetry from the schools: for in all seriousness it were better that a mill-stone were hanged about our necks and we drowned

[1] Such explanations defeat all the higher aims, by dragging the mind down from the realm of the imagination into the everyday world of facts; they take the attention from the *poetic* aspect of things to direct it to the *material*.

in the sea than that we should continue, as we have done in the past, to make poetry a task and a trouble. But it is not so. Children are naturally good critics of poetry, for they are akin to the poet, who is the child of the race; and they have an instinctive appreciation of its beauty—what other meaning has that poem which is the crown of Wordsworth?

To develop this critical instinct, to reveal it as a means of culture within reach of the very poorest, and as naturally leading on to interest in other arts, is the purpose of our poetry lessons. These notes are the record of my own attempts to fulfil that purpose.

1922 B

CHAPTER I

WHAT IS POETRY?

'May God make this world, my child, as beautiful to you as it has been to me.'—BLAKE, in old age.

'He beholds the light and whence it flows,
He sees it in his joy.'

WHAT poetry is, in spite of all the definitions, we can no more define than we can define life or love; but what things are poetry we know, as we know what things are living, and loving, by their attributes and by their effects upon us. And the first of these is a troubling of the waters of the spirit: all poetry expresses some one's feelings, and attempts to awaken the corresponding emotions in the heart of another.

All of us are poets in a measure because all of us have feeling, and power to communicate what we feel to others; but those we call poets are at once more sensitive, with a wider range of feeling; and better able to express what they feel, and move others to share their feelings. To speak in metaphor, the senses of their soul are more numerous and more acute, and their voices have a greater compass than is in common men. All of us, for example, see dimly, as a half-blind man sees a light, beauty in a hill or a cloud or a primrose; but the poet sees it as a radiant glow that moves him to cry aloud with delight and so to make us also look again more earnestly to share his vision. We hear, as a deaf man is conscious of a voice, the echo of music in running water; but he hears the full clear melody and calls to us to listen more intently that we too may catch it. We all have wondered vaguely at the mystery and the majesty of the stars, but he falls on his face before them and priest-like prays us, as many as hear him, to accompany him to the throne of heavenly grace, and to say after him words that once spoken are felt to be the only ones worthy, yet such as we ourselves could never have found. And in many places where there is a shy and subtle beauty that most of us would never see, a poet's eye discovers it and his voice makes it plain to us.

If the inventors of machinery, as Samuel Butler says, have given mankind supplementary, extra-corporeal limbs, the poets have a far nobler gift for us: they have opened new windows in our souls.

The greatest poet is he who has felt the most of all the things that move the hearts of men and felt them most deeply; and can touch the most hearts to sympathy. And that is why Shakespeare, whose heart was made out of the hearts of all humanity and whose tongue had learned all human speech, sits and smiles alone; and that is why we call him God-like.

As in all vital matters—and poetry is a vital matter—instinct plays a large part in recognition of what is good; and with children especially. But the condition of man's advance has been the sacrifice of instinct to judgement; and so children have to learn to know poetry by criticism as well as by intuition; for what is called the critical instinct in adults is really habit.

That it should be an attempt to communicate a genuine emotion is the first condition of poetry. But our hearts are hard and our senses dull compared with a poet's; and sometimes we are moved without being conscious of it. Emotion, then, will not always be our guide—except to the very highest poetry. We must learn to recognize it by its attributes and its outward form. There are no poetical *subjects*—there are indeed no artistic subjects, for art can find and reveal an aspect of beauty in everything that God has permitted to exist. It is not the thing but the saying that moves us, not the matter but the manner of its presentation. Poetry shows us an aspect of a thing, not the thing itself, which, as we know from Plato, we never can see as it really is; science shows us another aspect; religion another; common sense, perhaps, another.

On the high road near my house is a row of ancient cottages falling into decay, dark and dirty and really unfit for human habitation; in the daytime an eyesore and a reproach. Yet at night, when the beams of powerful car-lights fall on their tall fronts, they are transfigured and glow with a strange and weird beauty like the glamour of a dream. So art can make sad things beautiful, and sordid things wonderful, as in Mr. Hardy's novels.

Why this should be so is a question that would lead us into the deepest of all problems, the nature of good and evil. Can that be really ugly that may sometimes appear beautiful? Must not the beauty be there always, though we cannot see it? What was the vision that made Keats say

> There is a budding morrow in midnight?

Mr. G. K. Chesterton, in his clever attack on Mr. Hardy's art, assumes with Matthew Arnold that art should 'show us things as they are'; but art has nothing to do with the truth of things as they are, but with the impression they make on the artist's mind; sincerity we may demand from the artist but not truth, for who knows what is truth outside the narrow limits of mathematical science? Art is the expression of the artist's mood, not the representation of objective fact. To a poet in a lover's mood the sea smiles with him in his joy, the winds whisper the name of his beloved, the stars look down on him like friendly eyes; to the same poet, in another mood, the same sea looks grim and cruel, the winds mock his sighs, and the cold stars watch him with a passionless inscrutable gaze.

The gloom of Egdon Heath, the baseness of Sinister Street, the cruelty of Lear's daughters are not *facts*, but as subjective as Christmas at Dingley Dell or the Forest of Arden or things seen in a dream; but, like the things in dreams, they are more real than reality: they move us with more poignant emotions; while they are with us we enjoy a more concentrated experience; they make us live more poetically, while the mood they communicate endures.

But the actors are all spirits and soon

> Are melted into air, into thin air
>
> . . . . . .

And we are awake again to that other aspect of things which we call reality:

> Dreams, indeed, they are; but such as even
> Jove might dream.

Criticism is the study of the art by which the poet presents the emotional aspects of things so as to communicate his own feelings to others.

Emotion is not poetry, but the cause of poetry; and emotional expression is only poetry when it takes a beautiful form. Here again we are faced with the indefinable: we can only say that certain men have innate power to produce under the influence of emotion sounds and sights that thrill the senses of other men, and that the exercise of that power is called art—music, painting, sculpture, perhaps, acting. To exist as poetry, emotion must be translated into music and visual images, clear and beautiful; they may be terrible or saddening, but still beautiful; for it has been said that the greatest mystery of poetry is its power to invest the saddest things with beauty. When emotion takes an inartistic form, the result is not poetry but a sort of echo of poetry, sometimes so like the real thing that only a cultivated taste can distinguish between them. Then why trouble to do so? I cannot too strongly affirm that only by such trouble and training can we appreciate art at all or get any real good from it. 'We needs must love the highest when we see it': that applies to God alone and not to the works of any of His creatures. But if 'appreciate' be substituted for 'see', then it is true of art.

The echo of poetry awakes not emotion but that shadow of emotion, sentimentalism; usually as harmless as it is useless; but capable of becoming, when indulged, the most pernicious influence that can enter the heart of man. The most infamous name in human history is his who died with the words on his lips, 'What an artist perishes in me!' So have other sentimentalists deluded themselves, even in our own time. Criticism of letters, the effort to realize a genuine emotion, as Voltaire said, and Cicero before him, 'nourishes the soul, strengthens its integrity, furnishes a solace to it'; but an uncritical susceptibility to mere sentiment is more dangerous than the craving for strong drink.

This matter is of such vital importance to my point of view that unless I succeed in making it clear and carrying the reader with me, the rest of my labour will be lost. I will try to explain by an example. Eliza Cook's verses on 'The Old Arm-Chair' have been familiar to three generations:

> I love it, I love it, and who shall dare
> To chide me for loving that old arm-chair?
> I've treasured it long, as a sainted prize,
> I've bedewed it with tears and embalmed it with sighs;
> 'Tis bound by a thousand links to my heart;
> Not a tie will break, not a link will start.
> Would ye learn the spell? A mother sat there.
> And a sacred thing is that old arm-chair.

That is the attempt to express a real emotion, one of the deepest and purest that the heart can know, the loving remembrance of a dead mother. Yet somehow it misses the emotions and only awakens sentiment; sentimental minds may not be aware of the difference; but it does not 'tell' with most of us. The reason is that the form, the medium of expression, is not adequate to convey, to communicate, the emotion.

First, and most significant, it is lacking in musical power; I shall try to examine later on the technique of musical lines, but in the present instance the ear alone is a sufficient guide, and it *feels* these verses to have no adequate volume of sound to impart a strong emotion and no cadences to voice a deep one. If the verses are read aloud and then immediately afterwards

> O that those lips had language! Life has passed
> With me but roughly since I heard thee last.
> Those lips are thine—thy own sweet smile I see,
> The same, that oft in childhood solaced me;
> Voice only fails, else how distinct they say
> 'Grieve not, my child, chase all thy fears away!'
> The meek intelligence of those dear eyes
> (Blest be the art that can immortalize,
> The art that baffles Time's tyrannic claim
> To quench it) here shines on me still the same—

'The Old Arm-Chair' will sound like a mere jingle by the side of the solemn and deep musical note of Cowper's lines; yet the same emotion inspired both. Each is written in riming couplets with ten syllables to the line; but one rattles along with a bounce and a jerk: the other has a slow, grave movement befitting its sad reflective theme. Shall we say that Cowper loved his mother more deeply than Eliza Cook loved her's? I believe that not the depth of emotion but the power to transmute it into music, the command of the emotional medium, constitutes the real difference. Words may be but a tinkling cymbal even when there *is* love.

But, secondly, the visual images, the pictures, in 'The Old Arm-Chair' are vague and indefinite; we are not *made* to see them; and if we wish to do so we must construct them for ourselves 'from information received'. Then we have to view an old arm-chair as 'a prize'—an unusual rôle for a piece of second-hand furniture to play; and as it has been 'bedewed', a risk to which indoor effects are not meant to be subjected nor formed to sustain, it is not likely to excite much competition even though its being 'embalmed' (but 'sighs' are a poor preservative) might seem to warrant its durability. But whoever wins this prize must apparently take the lady as well; for it 'is bound by a thousand links to her heart', not one of which will break. One line of Cowper, 'The meek intelligence of those dear eyes', has more worth for the imagination than this whole stanza. I should be very sorry to make fun of a daughter's love for her dead mother. I am trying to show that the form of emotional expression does not convey the real emotion, and that those who fancy themselves 'moved' by it are from laziness or carelessness taking the shadow for the substance and deluding themselves with mere words. By such readers the publishers of feuilletons grow rich; worse still, a sense of unreality gradually grows upon them—for Eliza Cook's verses are much nearer the real thing than the great mass of bad verse—and then they assume that all poetry is an echo and a fiction, and cease to read it in any form. I fancy that people who have no taste for poetry fall roughly into two classes, those who have been fed on sentiment till they sickened of it, and those who have been crammed with notes on meanings and allusions and grammatical examples and biographical records until they have learned to curse the poets and all their works.

But neither of these classes has known poetry at all. I am not going to add another failure to the many attempts at defining what in its very essence is undefin able: but on the tomb of Lord Falkland's grandfather in Burford Church is an epitaph written by his wife; it concludes with a quatrain which always to me seems to express in poetry of the tenderest beauty the most essential truth about poetry:

> Love made me poet
> And this I writt,
> My harte did doe yt,
> And not my witt.
> . . . .

A poet, by his very name, is a 'maker': a maker of music, and of pictures; and in both, to some extent, a maker of the material—viz. language—in which he works.

CHAPTER II

RHYTHM AND RIME

As yet a child, nor yet a fool to fame,
I lisped in numbers, for the numbers came.

AND first of Music. Every one, almost, finds pleasure in music; yet delight in poetry is an enjoyment revealed but to a happy few; so that I have known a professed lover of music whose knowledge of poetry was limited to a line or two of Shakespeare's description of 'the man that hath no music in himself', with which he used to taunt people who had not learned to play the piano. The first and most fatal mistake we can make in regard to poetry is to forget that poetry was born of music and is a form of music. Its first appeal is through the ear direct to the emotions. It is to this extent a universal language, like all the fine arts. The sonorous flow of Greek verse, the stately rhythm of Latin, the subtle grace of French, have power to communicate the emotion of the poet quite apart from the literal meaning of his words. Repeated experiments have shown that children not only enjoy listening to the music of poetry in an unknown tongue, but that they are keenly responsive to its emotional appeal. 'Aux armes, citoyens! Formez vos bataillons' will stir them as a trumpet-call; the hiss of 'qu'un sang impur abreuve nos sillons!' needs no translation to be recognized as a curse; nor the lingering pathos of 'miserere Domine' as a prayer.

Those who have not made such experiments will be

astonished by children's intuitive insight into the meaning of mere sound—unless they happen to have really loved a dog. I lately heard a 'Greats' man read a passage of Homer to some boys of twelve, who knew no language but their own; they listened breathlessly and then told him that there had been a challenge, a fight, and a song of triumph—which was really the 'substance' of the passage. He then read some lines of Vergil, and they said 'it was a cavalry charge'; 'passer mortuus est' of Catullus, and they suggested that 'some one was speaking of a dead child'. Ages before articulate speech existed emotion was expressed and communicated in sound, and in poetry it still is so communicated, apart from the mere dictionary meaning of the words used.

I once asked a boy the meaning suggested by the sound of

Tendebantque manus ripae ulterioris amore

and he said he thought it was a part of the psalm that tells how by the waters of Babylon they sat down and wept.

It will usually be found that people who do not care for poetry have never learned to listen for the music in it, often have never realized that it is there. This, then, must be our first aim: to reveal poetry as melody and to help the children to read it musically, almost as one teaches them to read the melody of a musical score; not necessarily aloud at first, for young voices have not the necessary range or power to express their ideal, but to help them to make its music sound in the inward ear as one helps them to make its pictures flash upon the inward eye.

Rhythm and rime are the most obvious elements in the music of verse, and children must be taught to mark them, to bring them out and make them tell. The tendency to 'sing-song', which many teachers are apt to check, is a perfectly natural one—it lies at the very root of poetry—and the opposite extreme, poetry read in a light, snip-snap, conversational tone, controlled only by punctuation like the plainest prose, is far more offensive to a cultivated ear—and also to the natural ear. If any one will read—say—Blake's 'Little lamb, who made thee?' to a young child not yet sophisticated by school, first as prose and then with the rhythm marked even to sing-song and pausing at the ends of the lines, to mark the rimes regardless of punctuation, he will be left in no doubt as to which rendering the natural ear prefers. And instinct is a guide we ought never to disregard. We are told again and again in Lord Tennyson's *Memoir* that when Tennyson recited his own poems he almost intoned or chanted them, 'mouthing out his hollow oes and aes', and Hazlitt tells us the same of both Wordsworth and Coleridge. What we have to teach children is that their reading must satisfy alike the ear and the mind, both the demand of the sense for music and of the intellect for logic. But, for children at least, the first is by far the more important—and by far the less considered as a rule.

How rhythm and 'the jingling of like endings' affect the nervous system, and why certain sounds are pleasing to the ear, are ultimately physiological questions but, I believe, have not yet been explained; of smells, of course, biologists know more and can explain their 'survival values'. Men in a state of emotion tend naturally to speak rhythmically; the explanation may prove to be connected with the nervous control of the breath. Rhythm appears to be an attribute of life: wherever a heart beats or breath is drawn it is present.

Verse probably had its origin in meaningless sounds spontaneously uttered to accompany the rhythm of primitive dances; a great deal of early verse, e. g. folk songs, consists more or less largely of 'nonsense rhythm', like 'hey nonny oh nonny nonny nonny oh!' 'ri fol ri fol down-derry dey doh ri fol ri fol dee'. Then words without much 'content of thought' were chosen instead to fit the rhythm, and so began the earliest form of ballad—in schools, now happily growing more common, where dancing is taught, the practice of accompanying the dance by song might also be revived to the greater delight of the children: I know at least one school where folk dances, quadrilles, and lancers are always accompanied by the singing of nursery rimes or nonsense jingles. But words as spoken have a rhythm of their own which does not always correspond with the regular alternate beats of 'nonsense verse'; when we disregard this 'speech-rhythm' for the sake of the regular 'verse-rhythm' we have 'sing-song'. For example, the verse-rhythm in

˘ ¯ ˘ ¯ ˘ ¯ ˘ ¯
To-morrow is our wedding day
˘ ¯ ˘ ¯ ˘ ¯
And we will then repair
˘ ¯ ˘ ¯ ˘ ¯ ˘ ¯
Unto the Bell at Edmonton
˘ ¯ ˘ ¯ ˘ ¯
All in a chaise and pair

would please the ear but offend the reason because it fails to recognize the rhythm of speech—in singing, of course, we are content to do so because we seek to gratify the ear alone. But by slightly modifying this rendering, shifting a beat or dropping one here and there, yet still retaining a sufficiently regular fall to *suggest* the verse-rhythm, we may effect a compromise that will meet both demands:

˘ ¯ ˘ ˘ ˘ ¯ ˘ ¯
To-morrow is our wedding day
˘ ˘ ˘ ¯ ˘ ¯
And we will then repair
¯ ˘ ˘ ¯ ˘ ¯ ˘ ˘
Unto the Bell at Edmonton
¯ ˘ ˘ ¯ ˘ ¯
All in a chaise and pair.

It is of course the ear-pleasing verse-rhythm that we seek to keep near, and this is the more easy because speech-rhythm in phrases is less fixed and rigid, and so often offers alternatives one of which may be not far removed from verse-rhythm; for example in the line

˘ ¯ ˘ ¯ ˘ ¯
Or let me sleep alway

where the verse-rhythm is as marked, the speech-rhythm may be:

¯ ˘ ˘ ¯ ¯ ˘
Or let me sleep alway

or

˘ ¯ ˘ ¯ ¯ ˘
Or let me sleep alway

and we choose the second alternative as better allowing the verse-rhythm to be heard as the 'base music' of the line. When a line is written with so little art that no compromise is possible without sensible loss to one or other of the rhythms, we get doggerel:

˘ ¯ ˘ ¯ ˘ ¯ ˘ ¯ ˘ ¯
A Mister Wilkinson, a clergyman

is a well-known example: it we mark the verse-rhythm it is mere sing-song; but if we give it speech-rhythm

⏑ ⏑ ⏑ – ⏑ ⏑ ⏑ – ⏑ ⏑
A Mister Wilkinson, a clergyman,

all suggestion of a 'dance of numbers' disappears; not only so, but we can find no means of modifying the two rhythms to make them approach one another sufficiently to restore the suggestion of a regular beat. On the other hand in Hudibras, much of which is doggerel, the short, strong verse-rhythm is powerful enough to override the speech-rhythm. Doggerel is in Touchstone's phrase 'the very false gallop of verses'.

If the reader will experiment with other lines, of blank verse particularly, he will discover that this compromise between verse-rhythm and speech-rhythm is not merely a means of reconciling the conflicting demands of mind and sense, but is the source of a new and endless delight: it offers an almost infinite variety to the ear that would otherwise be tired and satiated by the very regularity for which it craves. The contrast between the two rhythms, with the resulting relief afforded by the constant necessity to vary the verse-rhythm in different ways, is indeed the one thing that enables the poet to maintain his readers' delight throughout a long poem. Gray's *Elegy*, fine poetry though it is, falls below the highest partly for this reason; he has been so careful to maintain the regularity of the verse-rhythm by choosing speech-rhythm that almost always corresponds, that towards the end, in spite of the beautiful imagery, we are beginning to be faintly conscious of a feeling of monotony. Those who habitually read poetry only for its ideas may dissent; but I believe that the music-lovers, to whom poetry is melody first, will agree that there is 'too much of a good thing' in the unvarying regularity of metre in the *Elegy*.

With Shakespeare, on the other hand, 'the thought constructs the tune, so that reading for the sense will best bring out the rhythm'; he leaves the verse-rhythm to take care of itself—which in his hands it always does, rippling along like a deep under-current. If the reader will turn to *Henry VIII*, iii. 2, where Shakespeare's work is mixed with Fletcher's, and will begin at line 351, he will find that the twenty lines of Wolsey's soliloquy are set to a regular verse-rhythm, so that they can easily be read as a 'sing-song' by any one who tries:

> Vain pomp and glory of this world, I hate ye:
> I feel my heart new-opened. O! how wretched
> Is that poor man that hangs on princes' favours!
> There is, betwixt that smile we would aspire to,
> That sweet aspect of princes, and their ruin,
> More pangs and fears than wars or women have——

That is Fletcher, though it is often learned by small boys as 'a Shakespearian gem'.

Now, at line 374 enters Shakespeare:

> Never so truly happy, my good Cromwell.
> I know myself now; and I feel within me
> A peace above all earthly dignities,
> A still and quiet conscience. The king has cur'd me,
> I humbly thank his Grace;——

The verse-rhythm has ceased to be insistent; it has sunk into subconsciousness; to read the rest of the scene in 'sing-song' is impossible without constantly doing violence to the sense. For though there *is* a rhythmic tune the sense has made it.

Teaching children to read verse so as to make it a delight to themselves and others, means, very largely, teaching them to mark the verse-rhythm, and at the same time avoid sing-song by modifying it where speech-rhythm dictates. It also means helping them to appreciate and render the full musical value of rime.

Rime is the one beauty in words which was not revealed to the Greeks. Like Gothic architecture, it is a gift conceived in France and developed by the western nations under French leadership. It was meet that it should come into England with the law and organization of the Conqueror, for it is a natural source—as he was and his race—of order and organized form. It brought the stanza into being, as he the state, and gave it definite shapes, as the mighty Norman hand formed lawless elements into the union of regular communities. An ill-instructed genius like Walt Whitman may preach and practise an ignorant contempt for rime as 'a feudal superstition', and inartistic minds who read him only for the substance of his thoughts may believe him. But without rime and its restricting and shaping control only the very greatest have power to force verse into the mould of beauty; and without rhythm poetry soon degenerates into the chaos of anarchy; for

> Rimes the rudders are of verses
> With which like ships they steer their courses.

The ear has an unexplained but natural delight in

them and listens for a rime as children listen for an echo, and, like them too, is the more delighted when the gratification is repeated; that is the great charm of the perfect sonnet-form. The simplest and probably the earliest use of rime is when two lines are associated by the bond of a similar ending to form the stanza or poetic unit called a couplet. But this is too cheap and obvious a gratification; it satisfies desire too soon. A great part of the pleasure given by rime to a cultured ear lies in the expectation of it. So the enjoyment of food, speaking generally, bears relation to the time one has been hungry. That is one reason why people now read Pope only for his philosophy and wit, and do not read his disciples' couplets at all.[1] The early couplet was shorter than Pope's, with only two or three stresses between the rimes:

> Violette y fut moult belle
> Et aussi parvenche nouvelle
>
> . . . .
>
> Si estoit soef flairans
> Et reflagrans et odorans.

The first advance was to lengthen the interval by increasing the number of stresses; and then, to avoid lines of unwieldy length, to break each one into two, and produce a quatrain of blank and riming lines alternating.

> – Sumer is icumen in,
> *a* Lhude sing cuccu!
> – Groweth sed and bloweth med,
> *a* And springth the wude nu.

[1] The riming in Browning's beautiful 'Love among the Ruins'—

> Where the quiet-coloured end of evening smiles
> Miles on miles . . .

does not form couplets because there are no stresses to make an interval between the rimes; sound and echo are practically simultaneous.

Soon an additional delight was devised by means of new rimes at the ends of the blank lines, interwoven with the original pair:

> *a* J'ai un roi de Cecile
> *b* Veu devenir berger,
> *a* Et sa femme gentille
> *b* De ce propre mestier.

Then a fifth line, echoing one of the pairs, or a couplet with a similar echo or with a fresh pair was added to the quatrain. Chaucer's most characteristic stanza combines both these additions:

> In hir is heigh beautee, withoute pryde, *a*
> Yowthe, withoute grenehede or folye; *b*
> To alle hir werkes vertu is hir gyde, *a*
> Humblesse hath slayn in hir al tirannye. *b*
> She is mirour of alle curteisye; *b*
> Hir herte is verray chambre of holinesse, *c*
> Hir hand ministre of fredom for almesse. *c*

Or the quatrain was treated as a half-stanza and another half was composed to correspond, which could of course be done in a great variety of ways, e. g.:

> *a* There star nor sun shall waken,
> *b* Nor any change of light,
> *a* Nor sound of waters shaken,
> *b* Nor any sound or sight;
> *c* Nor wintry leaves nor vernal,
> *c* Nor days nor things diurnal,
> *c* Only the sleep eternal
> *b* In an eternal night.

So in rime the stanza had its origin and through the

various possibilities of rime-arrangement was developed, until from it in turn grew the sonnet, the noblest piece of verbal architecture that the mind of man has conceived. I shall return to the subject of rimes and rhythms in considering stanza-forms in a later chapter; at present I am mainly concerned to show that the delight of poetry is primarily a sensuous one—that it has a natural power to charm, independent of the meaning of its words. For I believe this conception to be at once most vital to fruitful study and teaching and least realized in the schools and training colleges.

CHAPTER III

POETRY IS MUSIC

'Bid me discourse: I will enchant thine ear.'

'Repeat me these verses again . . . for I always love to hear poetry twice, the first time for sound and the latter time for sense.'

THERE is a much finer and a more subtle music in poetry than the mere rhythm and rimes of verse can impart. It lies in the poet's choice of melodious words and in their harmonious arrangement; it is a charm common as well to prose as to poetry, and is the secret of greatness, of 'the grand style', in both.

But it is a beauty as ethereal as it is subtle, and its appreciation depends almost absolutely on perfect intonation and accent in rendering it. It is the nearest realized as we best succeed in approaching the sound the poet heard in the inward ear as he composed his lines—every vowel with its full value; every consonant, especially the terminals, clear; the l's liquid; the r's trilled, gently but perceptibly; and yet without any unnaturalness and obvious effort or suggestion of 'prunes and prisms'. No easy matter all this for most of us in these 'derderderderdy' days. Above all, the pitch of the voice is important; the light head-voice of colloquial speech—in which children are too often taught to read for the sake of what is believed to be 'expression'—would utterly abolish and destroy the beauty of the finest line. The musical charm of poetry depends almost as much upon tone and enunciation in the reader as that of music itself does upon perfect tune in the instrument. Poetry in slovenly or perverted speech is as excruciating to a sensitive ear as a song on a gramophone.

I think we shall better reveal to children the music in good verse, and train them to 'sound' it mentally, by frequently reading, or better still, reciting to them poems whose music we ourselves by loving study have learned to feel, than by requiring them, especially in class, to read or recite aloud. When we have made music for them, and they have learned to love it and look for it, they will want to make oral music for themselves, to use their voices as instruments to express the melody they *feel* in poetry—

> That mind and *voice* according well
> May make one music.

But, at first, the more they feel the less ready will they be to give their feeling utterance aloud in class. Individual help, difficult as it is in the battalion-classes of our barrack schools, is the best way to encourage confidence and secure correct and musical rendering.

I believe there is far too much reading aloud in the primary schools; we learn to read mainly for personal and private enjoyment and not, unless we are parsons, for public edification: this is not selfishness, but common sense. Constant reading aloud in youth tends to slow the thoughts and may result in a confirmed habit of muttering when one is reading to himself, which is next door to idiocy, and is also a deplorable waste of nervous energy.

Moreover, the voices of younger children, at least, are quite incompetent to render fine poetry so as to give pleasure to others: they know it; and they have told me again and again that they can 'sound it in their heads but cannot say it'. If we were not so possessed by the evil spirit of Examinable Results, we should know that physical organs can never perfectly render the ideal conception, and that music in the brain is a far better thing than music on the tongue.

It is of the highest importance to train children to distinguish between the swing and jingle of mere verse and the finer music of poetry, between e.g. O'Shaughnessy's 'We are the Music-makers' and 'Casabianca'; to help them to compare the sound, the melody, apart from the matter. The presence of incident in 'Casabianca' will tend to corrupt their judgement. But I believe that the natural ear is an instinctive guide, and that if good and bad verse are read one after the other, most children, unless their ear has already been spoilt, will prefer the good.

I suggest that we should frequently select poems for reading or recitation to the children solely for their beauty of music; that we should neither ask ourselves whether children are likely to 'understand' them, nor them whether they do. We do not always ask what a piece of music 'means'—though we might do so more frequently; we are content to listen 'in a wise passiveness', or even to enjoy a purely sensuous pleasure. And though such enjoyment is only a *part* of the delight of poetry, yet it is an essential part; and in order to help them to feel it we should do well to read them Swinburne as we might read them Catullus, for the beauty of sound alone.

I have found that children enjoy the music of the Milking Song, in Jean Ingelow's 'High Tide', when it is well recited, as much as they enjoy a fine song; they like Tennyson's 'Frater, Ave atque Vale', though they certainly cannot understand the words; and when I ask them what poem they would like to hear they often ask for 'The Northern Farmer' or William Barnes's 'Wife A-lost' or 'Blackmwore Maidens', though the dialects are largely unintelligible in Oxfordshire.

The art which creates that diviner music that seems independent of the mechanism of prosody is the gift of the great poets and sometimes seems beyond the reach of criticism, the effect of magic or inspiration. Yet it *is* art, and as such depends upon a technique whose secrets are not all past our study.

The use of alliteration, for example, can be noted and appreciated even by the younger children; not the cheaper and more obvious device of head-rime only, at which Shakespeare laughs in

> Whereat with blade, with bloody blameful blade,
> He boldly broached his boiling bloody breast,

but his own subtle and secret effects that we enjoy without observing the means until we look for them:

> O *m*ist*r*e*ss* *m*ine, whe*r*e a*r*e you *r*oa*m*ing?
> O, *s*tay and hea*r*! you*r* t*r*ue *l*ove'*s* co*m*ing,
> That can *s*ing both high and *l*ow——

alliteration that is like the beauty of shot silk.

The effect of hard and soft consonants can also be studied. When our ears, with the Ancient Mariner's, are

> Stunned by that loud and dreadful sound
> Which sky and ocean smote

suddenly follows a hush

> And all was still save that the hill
> Was telling of the sound.

The contrast itself is the highest art; but the *means* by which it is wrought is art also. It lies partly in the numerous mutes, 'consonantal sounds produced by the sudden and forcible interruption of the passage of the breath', of the first description—the final *d*'s and *t*'s and in the explosive *f*; and in the liquids and sibilants of which the second is full.

It lies, too, in the choice of vowel-sounds, to which Tennyson attached so much importance: most of the vowels in the first passage are long and open, *ō*'s and *ou*'s, full of sound; most in the second are short and closed, *ă*'s and *ĭ*'s and *ĕ*'s.

Tennyson's 'secret' of varying vowel-sounds can be found and studied in every great musical line—

> 1 2 3 4 5 6 7 8 6 9
> And leaping down the ridges lightly, plunged
> 1 10 5 11 9 7 1 9 5 12
> Among the bulrush beds, and clutched the sword
> 1 13 14 1 15 6
> And strongly wheeled and threw it . . .

In less than three lines, taken not from the book but from memory at random, the first that came to mind, there are fifteen different vowel-sounds, and only five of them occur more than once, and then not in juxtaposition.

The original verse of the children will afford examples for discussion of the discord produced by neglect of this artistic 'canon'—there is an instance in the clash of 'sounds' and 'found' a few lines above, which, now that I have noticed it, may stand as an example. I will quote one from a poet more often guilty of such blemishes than the enthusiasm of some of his admirers would have us believe.

1 2 3 4 5 1 6 7 6 1
Lift not thy hands to it [heaven] for help for it
8 1 2 7 1 2 4 9 6 3
Rolls impotently on as thou or I.

There we have but nine variations of vowel-sounds in twenty; one of them is repeated five times, two others thrice each; the lack of music in the first line, especially, would strike an organ-blower.

Another source of music is to be found in the harmony, in the literal sense of the word, that results from the apposition of words of different lingual origin—the long rolling Latin and Greek polysyllables contrasting with the more numerous stresses of the short Anglo-Saxon words:

> Not *marble* nor the gilded *monuments*
> Of *princes* shall outlive this *powerful* rime.

It is one of the secrets of the music in the English Prayer-book and particularly of the consummate prose of the Litany:

> That it may *please* Thee to *preserve* all that *travel* by land or by water, all women *labouring* of child, all sick *persons*, and young children; and to shew thy *pity* upon all *prisoners* and *captives*.

Much cant has been written about this 'device', often by people who suppose that any monosyllable is Saxon; on the other hand, it is often held too cheap by scholars who remember that 'a little learning is a dangerous thing' because a scholar said it, and forget that 'half a loaf is better than no bread' because it is vulgar wisdom.

Consciously used as an artifice it always fails, and it is insufficient, alone, to explain the finest music—

> The *uncertain glory* of an April day.

Substitute other Romance words, as 'varying' and 'splendour' for 'uncertain' and 'glory', and the magic of the music disappears. But the fact remains that in most fine lines the two elements are to be found.

One cannot imagine a more interesting introduction to etymology than the attempt to distinguish the interwoven strains that combine to make the harmony of verse.

I should be sorry to be thought for a moment to suggest that any great poet ever wrote with definite 'rules' or 'artistic canons' in mind: works of art are not composed in that way; instinct, the gift of the poet's ear, are alone his guides. But though works of art are not made by rule, yet rules may be made from them; certain definite touchstones and principles can be found in fine work, and we know that Tennyson for instance, when his poem was finished, examined it by the light of them. He knew, for example, that the excess of sibilants in English is a source of hissing, and he carefully went through his work to rid it of this element—he called it 'kicking the geese out of the boat'. But he knew too that the use of esses in hushing a passage to suit a quiet theme is a most valuable resource in our language—

> Mu*s*ic that bring*s* *s*weet *s*leep down from the bli*ss*ful *s*kie*s*,
> Mu*s*ic that gentlier on the *s*pirit lie*s*
> Than tir'd eyelid*s* upon tir'd eye*s*.

What lullaby was ever more soothing? The eyelids droop as one quotes.

Most beautiful effects are obtained by this means. And that *s* is in itself unmusical a single quatrain of Shakespeare is sufficient to disprove:

When to the sessions of sweet silent thought
I summon up remembrance of things past,
I sigh a lack of many a thing I sought,
And with old woes new wail my dear time's waste.

One of the most wonderful lines in the world is made so by the poet's taking advantage of the very thing that has sometimes been held a fault in English:

O mors, quam amara est memoria tua homini pacem habenti
in *s*ub*s*tantii*s* *s*ui*s*!

There, surely, 'the music of silence speaks if it ever has spoken. The words seem to tremble back into the silence their whisper has interrupted.' The truth is that esses only hiss when a terminal *s* clashes with an initial one; Tennyson had this in mind when he said that his famous line

Freedom *s*lowly broaden*s* down . . .

often suffered by being misquoted with the esses in contact:

Freedom broaden*s* *s*lowly down.

Still less do I mean that criticism is a balance in which to weigh the infinite, a calculus by which small minds can sum up great ones; we must recognize with reverence that when criticism has said its last word there is something, there is much, still unexplained in great art. We know some words make music, 'almost singing themselves they run', but we often cannot say why; names, for example, like—

Blind Thamyris and blind Maeonides
And Tiresias and Phineus, prophets old

and

Ariel and Arioch and the violence
Of Ramiel . . .

and of heavenly handmaidens

Whose Names
Are five sweet symphonies,
Cecily, Gertrude, Magdalen,
Margaret and Rosalys.

Alter the order and you spoil the symphony: why? That we cannot always find an answer is no reason why we should not inquire. The superhuman is not really appreciated as divine until we have tried to measure it.

CHAPTER IV

SOUND AND SENSE

''Tis not enough no harshness gives offence,
The sound must seem an echo to the sense.'

'For if proper and naturall wordes in well joyned sentences do lyvely expresse the matter, let it be troublesome, quyet, angry or pleasant, a man shal thincke not to be readyng but present in doyng of the same.'

NEXT, and almost equal in importance to the music of poetry, is its power to suggest its meaning by its sound. We have touched on this matter several times already and we shall meet it again, for it is of the very essence of poetry. Children, particularly, should learn to look for it in every poem they study, not merely in single words, but, what is much more rare and beautiful, in sustained passages; for here, if anywhere, 'beauty is truth, truth beauty'.

I say children particularly because they are primitive people and this is an essentially primitive device, and one which never fails to delight them when they appreciate it—as they are wonderfully quick to do. A great part of language had its origin in attempts to imitate natural sounds, as of water, the wind, thunder, and the cries of animals. The Greek root *kăkè* for example, with its meaning of evil and worthless, suggests by its gutturals the sound one makes in rejecting from the palate some unpleasant thing taken into the mouth; and though it is not in the English dictionary it is almost identical in sound with the noise an English mother makes in teaching her baby that certain things are nauseous. So in most languages of western Europe the words for thunder are almost identical and are derived from the actual sound.

Such words belong to a stage of human evolution in

which man was an 'emotional' but not yet a 'reasoning' being, in which he apprehended sounds, as very young children and even the higher animals do, but did not comprehend them. Now poetry, which speaks primarily to that older, deeper, unchanging being in us, which we call the heart, is full of these primitive words that are of the instinct rather than of the understanding. Many of them, as we shall see later on of metaphors, have lost all trace of their origin, but their power is still latent in them and the poet calls it out. But he does more: what the primitive poets who first made language did for single words the later poets do for whole phrases; they charge them with the power to suggest at once the sound of things and the mood it produced in the hearer.

Nothing is more important in rendering poetry than to give the full emotional sound-value to such imitative words and passages. If a child does it in his reading there is no need to ask him—always a dangerous and often a deadly thing—to 'explain' the meaning.

This art of fusing sense in sound exists in varying degrees according as the veritable sound as well as the mood that accompanies it is more or less suggested. In all good poetry the *general* sound of a poem or passage corresponds with the mood in which it is written and which it is meant to communicate: we have found in this a test for 'The Old Arm-Chair' and we should always apply it. Is the music written in the right key? Thus Browning's song with its refrain:

> Marching along,
> Fifty score strong,
> Great-hearted Gentlemen
> Singing this song

has a hearty jovial sound in keeping with its sentiment and a short rapid swing corresponding to the action which it expresses. So Constable's

> Diaphenia like the daffadowndilly,
> White as the sun, fair as the lily;
> Heigh ho! how I do love thee

is light and airy, like his fancy—for it is only a fancy and not love—and comes trippingly off the tongue; while

> On Linden when the sun was low
> All bloodless lay the untrodden snow,
> And dark as winter was the flow
> Of Iser, rolling rapidly

has a deep solemn tone of 'old unhappy far-off things, and battles long ago'; and, not to multiply examples,

> Hame, hame, hame, O hame fain wad I be—
> O hame, hame, hame, to my ain countree!

breathes hopeless passion and yearning in every syllable.

We should always look for this general correspondence between mood and sound, for the quiet hushed words that speak of peaceful things, for the light phrases of gaiety, for the full sonorous 'noisy' words that tell of battle and tumult, for the long slow-footed rhythm of grief and lamentation.

Metre, as we have seen, and as we shall see more at large in the next chapter, accounts partly for these effects; the more the stresses in proportion to the number of syllables the slower the movement; Cowper had five stresses in ten syllables, Eliza Cook but four. Browning's 'Marching Along' has practically only one stress in a line—on the first syllable in each; the force of which is sufficient not only to give rhythm to the whole line, but to weaken the theoretical stress on the last syllable almost to vanishing point; Constable's 'Diaphenia' has only two, or at most three stresses, in his long lines of ten or twelve syllables. But in 'Hame, hame, hame' almost every syllable is stressed, and a *felt* sigh between them takes the place of the others.

The choice of vowels is almost equally important: long vowels slow the movement, short vowels quicken it. The third stanza of Wordsworth's 'Daffodils' is a good example:

> The waves beside them danced, but they
>   Outdid the sparkling waves in glee;
> A poet could not but be gay,
>   In such a jocund company:
> I gazed—and gazed—but little thought
> What wealth the show to me had brought.

The quatrain, with most of its vowels short, moves lightly like the flowers and waves of which it speaks; but the couplet with its long *a*'s and *aw*'s suddenly slows the movement down to correspond with the reflective mood with which the stanza ends. The contrast, alike between the sound of the fourth and fifth lines and the length of their vowels, should be particularly noticed.

Another fine example is Tennyson's:

> By the margin, willow-veil'd,
> Slidé the heavy barges, trail'd
> By slow horses; and unhail'd
> Thé shállóp flíttéth sílkén-sáil'd
>   Skímmíng dówn tó Cámélót.

The slow motion of the barges and horses is

marvellously suggested by the dragging movement of the long vowels in 'slide', 'barges', 'trail'd', 'by', 'slow', 'horses', while the short vowels in the last two lines wing the words so that they fly like the shallop. Here too the *h*'s help to slow the movement by their demands on the breath to mark them distinctly; so too, and for the same reason, do the terminal *d*'s in 'slide' and 'trail'd'; they cannot be said quickly without a slovenly slurring.

Again, in Shelley's

> Wild roses, and ivy serpentine
> With its dark leaves and buds wandering astray,

and in Tennyson's

> Overhead the wandering ivy and vine,

the rhythm suggests the waving and winding of the trailing plants. So Coleridge's

> One red leaf, the last of its clan,
> That dances as often as dance it can,
> Hanging so light and hanging so high,
> On the topmost twig that looks up at the sky—

does not dance more sprite-like than his numbers.

In criticism, as in biology, it is not only the adaptation of means to ends, of structure to function, that interests us; we have also to study the method by which such results are produced, to ask how? as well as why? We know, for example, by simple observation that most leguminous plants scatter their seeds afar by twisting their pods until the smooth, rounded seeds are squeezed and shot out by the pressure; but *how* that torsion is accomplished we can only discover by a microscopical examination of cell-tissues.

Failure to appreciate *how* an effect was produced, although he understood *why*, led Johnson astray in a well-known criticism on Pope's

> With many a weary step, and many a groan,
> Up a high hill he heaves a huge round stone·
> The huge round stone resulting with a bound,
> Thunders impetuous down and smokes along the ground.

'Who does not perceive the stone to move slowly upward and roll violently back?' says Johnson. 'But set the same numbers to another sense:

> While many a merry tale and many a song
> Cheered the rough road, we wished the rough road long;
> The rough road then returning in a round
> Mocked our impatient steps, for all was fairy ground.

We have now surely lost much of the delay and much of the rapidity,' and he then goes on to declare that 'Beauties of this kind are commonly fancied'. If he had used 'commonly' in the exact sense of the word, as a lexicographer should have done, he might have seen that what is perceived by all cannot be dismissed as fanciful—even by a Dictator who thought he had demolished Berkeley's whole philosophy by kicking his foot against a stone. But by neglecting to examine the *mechanism* of Pope's art he failed to see that he had produced his effect, partly by means of the difference between the sense-rhythm and the verse-rhythm; partly by using long vowels in the stressed words—'weary', 'groan', 'high', 'heaves', 'huge', 'round', and 'stone' in the upward movement, and short ones in the downward—'the', 'resulting', 'with', 'a', 'thunders', 'impetuous', and 'along'; and partly, very largely indeed.

by the repeated *h*'s in the second line suggesting the slow, panting effort of the toiler. In his parody he has omitted the most important of these devices; the sense-rhythm trips along with the verse-rhythm; he has no stressed long vowel in the whole of the first line and few short ones in the two last; he has got rid of all the aspirates and with them of the laborious effect of Pope's upward movement; and by the terminal *d*'s of his last two lines he has slowed the movement of that part. So he obtains the uniformity at which he aims. But contrast is as much a fact, and as much a matter of technique, in poetry as in painting.

But there is a further degree of onomatopoeic poetry in which not the mood only but the suggestion of the appropriate sound itself is produced by the words employed.

Professor Saintsbury has remarked that in the stanza

> The fair breeze blew, the white foam flew,
> The furrow follow'd free;
> We were the first that ever burst
> Into that silent sea

—the rush of the words corresponds with the swift movement they express. That is a fine example of general harmony between the subject and the sound; so is the quietness, the result of the esses, in the last line. But a boy of twelve lately suggested to me that, beyond this general correspondence, the actual sound of a keel forced swiftly through waves can be heard in the repeated *ff*'s! That is an example of the imitation of particular sounds.

I had not noticed it before; some ears may not hear

it now. But I thanked the boy and shall always be indebted to him for increasing my appreciation of Coleridge. It would be quite irrelevant to suggest that Coleridge never intended this effect; if he did not, which we hardly dare assume, he wrought, as all poets do, but better than he knew.

Let me say here, although I may be guilty of repeating myself in another chapter, that we should be scrupulously careful to receive with respect and encouragement any suggestion from children as to what a sound means to them, even though we ourselves do not hear the same. They are nearer the poet's heart, and perhaps nearer the truth of things, than we are; their intuition is often wiser than our wisdom. Out of the mouths of babes and sucklings may come the truest and subtlest criticism; it is the deep things that are often hidden from the wise and prudent and revealed unto babes. The little child is free of the kingdom of poetry as well as of the kingdom of heaven, and may lead us into it. Indeed I shall try to maintain that what was said of the condition of entry into the one kingdom applies also to the other.

But all this is from *our* point of view. Quite apart from our own advantage we ought to encourage children's ideas; for as Pater somewhere says: 'The salt of all aesthetic study is in the question—what, precisely what, does this mean for *me*?'; and as a greater than he has said:

> There is nothing, either good or bad,
> But thinking makes it so.

I dwell on this because I have found that nothing in poetry attracts children more, and nothing more excites them to spontaneous appreciation and criticism than that 'echo of the sense' which Dr. Johnson found 'fanciful', and which Dr. Hadow—it is true, only in a school-book—like him dismisses as 'tricks of descriptive music, a quip and a conceit . . . a mere jingle'. But when it is asserted that although 'Tennyson himself said that the couplet from "Birds in the High Hall Garden"

> Maud, Maud, Maud, Maud,
> They were crying and calling

was intended to represent the cawing of rooks. But we can hardly take this seriously', I can only think that the writers know no more of Tennyson than they do of birds: Tennyson was not in the habit of saying what he did not mean; and rooks *are* in the habit of saying, 'Maud, Maud, Maud', 'or', as Tennyson said, 'something very like it'.

Tennyson is the great modern master of suggestive sound; but he drew from ancient springs, closed alas to elementary schools, scholars and teachers, and, by the suicidal policy of the older universities, soon to be closed to the modern world; for optional Greek will lead to optional Latin, and then the last stronghold of liberal learning, where so many generations of men have learned the meaning of humanity, will be transformed into a great technical school where clerks learn book-keeping and druggists practise dispensing.

Andrew Lang tells us that Vergil was Tennyson's master; and we know from his own lips that 'the only good thing he got from school was the memory of the words "sonus desilientis aquae" and of an old wall, covered with weeds, opposite the school windows'; pregnant facts, both of them, to a student of Tennyson's poetry

Before I quote examples let me deplore the existence of the superior person who murmurs 'hackneyed' when famous lines are mentioned.

Great art can never be hackneyed in spite of the hacks;

> Age cannot wither her, nor custom stale
> Her infinite variety.

I know that has been quoted before, and I hope it will be quoted 'so long as men can breathe or eyes can see'. For those who love the poets, no less than they themselves, are

> For ever piping songs for ever new.

And it is because of their undamageable beauty and charm that miscalled hackneyed lines are constantly found

> Where breath most breathes—even in the mouths of men.

F. W. H. Myers once said that 'the highest use of language, of history itself, has been to bestow upon mankind a few thousand lines of poetry for which all other study of bygone ages is but practice and preparation, and which should become by endless broodings no mere acquisition from without, but the inmost structure and prepotent energy of the onward-striving soul'.

To have made even a little of 'the inner soul of poetry' a part of the texture of one's thought is a better thing than all a pedant's knowledge. Really to love the Ancient Mariner, for example, is alone a liberal education; it is to possess a sure touchstone of taste and a standard of literary worth. . . .

In 'The moan of doves in immemorial elms' as in Vergil's

> Nec gemere aëria cessabit turtur ab ulmo

we hear something more than a soothing sound in keeping with cooing; we have the voice of the dove itself speaking in music; and in

Murmuring of innumerable bees

there is, beside the drowsy sense of summer afternoons, the actual hum of insects. So when he tells us that

Miriam Lane
Made such a voluble answer promising all,

it is not the *sense* of the words but the *sound* of her breathless chatter that tells us most; and we have no need to translate the voice of the brook saying

I-babble-on-the-pebbles

into consciousness: the sound, not the words, tells what it is doing. Tennyson is very fond of reproducing the music of waters. He makes us hear

'The water lapping on the crag
And the long ripple washing in the reeds'.

'The scream of a maddened beach dragged down by the waves',

'The league-long roller thundering on the reef',

and the quiet breathing of a peaceful world in

Universal ocean softly washing all her warless isles.

But nothing that Tennyson ever did in this way is finer than Wordsworth's

What sorrow would it be
That mountain floods should thunder as before
And Ocean bellow from his rocky shore,
And neither awful voice be heard by thee!

To me, though it may be but a personal fancy, the *last* of those lines is the most wonderful. Coming after the roar of the torrent and the bellowing of the sea there seems in it the low, muttering echo that one hears as the voice of the thunder dies away.

One of the finest stanzas in Jean Ingelow's finest poem suggests its subject both by its rhythm and by the use of onomatopoeia:

> So farre, so fast the eygre drave,
> The heart had hardly time to beat
> Before a shallow, seething wave
> Sobb'd in the grasses at our feet:
> The feet had hardly time to flee
> Before it brake against the knee
> And all the world was in the sea.

Here the whispering esses in 'shallow', 'seething', 'sobb'd', and 'grasses', give the very sound of the stealthy waters creeping in the grass; and the swift rush of monosyllables in the next lines and the feeling of a great *force* in the last one—how accomplished I cannot tell—brings home to us by sound alone the irresistible advance of the flood.

I believe that whenever a great poet speaks of sounds he tries, consciously or unconsciously, to suggest them by the music of his verse—

> Methought the billows spoke and told me of it,
> The winds did sing it to me; and the thunder,
> That deep and dreadful organ pipe, pronounc'd
> The name.

He knows as well

> To tear with thunder the wide cheeks of the air

as to

> Kiss the wild waves whist,

to imitate the sound of

> A wind that shrills all night in a waste land

as of

> The swish of a skirt in the dew.

Where the subject is suitable sound-writing may often be sustained throughout a long passage or a whole poem. It is, naturally, in such a poem as Dryden's music Ode that we should look for an example. The opening lines

> In harmony, in heavenly harmony
> This universal frame began . . .

always make me think of an orchestral overture, and though that may be fanciful it is no fancy that in the succeeding stanzas the actual sounds of individual instruments are successively suggested, first—

> The trumpet's loud clangour
> Excites us to arms!
> With shrill notes of anger
> And mortal alarms,

then the big drum booms

> The double double double beat
> Of the thundering DRUM!

and the quick kettledrum rattles

> 'Tis-too-late-to-retreat,

then all is hushed while

> The soft complaining flute
> In dying notes discovers
> The woes of hapless lovers
> Whose dirge is whispered by the warbling lute.

and then, with a passionate outcry,

> Sharp violins proclaim
>   Their jealous pangs and desperation,
>   Fury, frantic indignation,
> Depth of pains and height of passion

if ever violins 'speak' they speak there; if the passage is properly rendered one hears their swift falsetto rise almost into a scream in 'desperA*tion*' 'indignA*tion*'.

But now the deep, full tones of 'the sacred organ',

> Notes inspiring holy love,
> Notes that wing their heavenly ways
> To mend the choirs above,

calm the unruly passions and lift the heart above.

Bell-music, perhaps from the simplicity of its rhythm, has often been imitated. Poe's poem is of course familiar, but Kipling's 'Bells and the Queen' is even closer to the sound of bells 'ringing down'. Swinburne's

> All the bells of heaven may ring

will give me an opportunity to emphasize the importance of careful study of a poem as a preliminary to reading it aloud: the line quoted might be read, and would be read by a casual eye, with no suggestion of bell-music; but the rhythm is there, and the line may, and should, be made to suggest a peal of bells running down an octave.

'The Charge of the Light Brigade' is a good example of sustained sound-writing. You hear the horses canter

> Half-a-league, | half-a-league, | half-a-league,

and then gallop:

> All-in-the | valley-of-death |
> Rode-the-six | hundred, |

you hear the roar of cannons and the confused hurly-burly of battle:

> Cannon to right of them,
> Cannon to left of them,
> Cannon in front of them,
>   Volleyed and thundered.
> . . . . .
> Flash'd all their sabres bare,
> Flash'd as they turn'd in air,
> Sabring the gunners there,

and then the halting retreat of tired and wounded horses as

> Then they rode back, | but not |
>   Not | the six hundred,

the repetition of the 'not' with the slowness due to the need to clear the *t*'s is almost the whole secret of the drag in these two lines.

But much finer than the 'Charge' is the end of the *Revenge*:

> They mann'd the Revenge with a swarthier alien crew,
> And away she sail'd with her loss and long'd for her own;
> When a wind from the lands they had ruin'd awoke from
>   sleep,
> And the water began to heave and the weather to moan,
> And or ever that evening ended a great gale blew,
> And a wave like the wave that is rais'd by an earthquake
>   grew,

Till it smote on their hulls and their sails and their masts
and their flags,
And the whole sea plunged and fell on the shot-shatter'd
navy of Spain,
And the little Revenge herself went down by the island crags
To be lost evermore in the main.

The poet, unlike the musician, has no 'marks of expression' to guide the beginner in rendering his work. If the use of musical terms be for once allowed for the sake of an example we might mark the first two lines piano or pianissimo, to suggest their burden of sadness; the next two lines will be crescendo, rising in the next lines to forte and fortissimo as the storm gathers and breaks and smites

On their hulls and their sails and their masts and their flags

(the repetition is again responsible for the effect of concentrated and growing energy); then, diminuendo, in the penultimate line, the force and fury die away, and the last line is pianissimo

The rest is silence.

It is to be noted that these sound-effects are not simply the result of selecting onomatopoeic words; Southey's 'Lodore', which we feel to be a mere *tour de force* and which leaves us cold, is evidence of this; it is simply a list of words made by prehistoric poets. But the great poets begin where the primitive onomatopoeia ends and fuse sense not into single sounds but into phrases. How they do it is often a mystery; yet we can sometimes

Watch
The Master work and catch
Hints of the proper craft, tricks of the tool's true play.

Some people may smile at this chapter as moonshine. And from their own point of view they will be perfectly right. For poetry *is* moonshine, that moonshine by which Lorenzo and Jessica looked at the world and in which all true lovers see it always ; and in the light of which Puck went about his business. May I have always glimpses of this light, and my boys and my readers.

Others, more learned, will contemn delight in imitative sound as love of jingle, primitive, barbarian. I am sure that no child will grow up to love poetry who has not first delighted in jingle. And for myself, if such enjoyment *is* primitive, I am content to remain a barbarian. Better a Barbarian than a Philistine.

CHAPTER V

STANZA-FORM

For of the soul the body form doth take,
For soul is form and doth the body make.

A GOOD deal may be done to develop the musical sense in children, and to help them to appreciate verbal melody, by examination of the architecture of verse. They should learn to count the 'beats' or stresses in the lines, and observe their relations to the unaccented syllables; e.g. they may be led to see that

– ◡ – ◡ – ◡ –
Twinkle, | twinkle, | little | star

runs lightly and quickly, partly because a beat is followed by an unaccented syllable: it 'trips from long to short'; while

◡ – ◡ – ◡ – ◡ –
The way | was long | the wind | was cold |

has a slower and graver movement, 'from short to long in solemn sort', partly due to the beats following the unaccented syllable (but the short and long vowels however have at least as much to do with this). I have marked off the syllables as 'feet' in the ancient manner, but children should not be troubled by the vexed question of quantities versus stresses involved in the use of the term foot, and they should learn to measure a line not by dividing it into compartments by vertical strokes but by placing a mark, e.g. a horizontal stroke, above the stressed syllables.

Again by increasing the number of beats, as in

> The curfew tolls the knell of parting day,

the slowing effect is increased, till with six stresses we get the Alexandrine line

> Which like a wounded snake, drags its slow length along.

And by decreasing the proportion of stresses, as in anapaestic and dactylic verse, the action is quickened; even the younger children can appreciate the swift movement in

> As I ride as I ride
> With a full heart for my guide
> As I ride as I ride,

and in

> Half a league, half a league.

I have found all this as simple as it is interesting to children; and, though no certificates are to be gained by it—a rare distinction for a subject in these days—it is an interest that will last when the fever and the fret of competitive examinations are over, and certificates have lost their charm; it will be a pleasure when the evil days come and it may serve us, more than most of our studies, in preparing for the final examination.

Plans of rime-arrangement are also very simple and interesting: rimes may be indicated by letters, and blanks by dashes:

> I know the way she went —
> Home with her maiden posy, *a*
> For her feet have touched the meadows —
> And left the daisies rosy. *a*

I think it is a good plan in writing rimed verse to arrange the lines so that the initial letters of the riming lines fall under one another, and similarly the initials of the blank lines; thus at a glance blank verse is distinguished from rimed, and the stanza-form is outlined. Moreover children are thus prevented from varying the stanza-form in their own verses, which in early attempts they always tend to do; they will rime their first stanza *a b a b* for example, and then in the second will forget the secondary rimes and write *—a—a*; or they will change from a quatrain to couplets, *a a b b*. But I hope to return to this in a chapter on original verse.

Children should be led to see that the rime arrangement that gives form to the stanza is neither haphazard nor arbitrary, but is purposely designed to please the ear, as I have shown when speaking of rime. One of the simplest examples of this is FitzGerald's stanza:

> Ah, Love, could thou and I with Fate conspire
> To grasp this sorry Scheme of Things entire,
>   Would we not shatter it to bits, and then
> Remould it nearer to the heart's desire!

The ear is gratified by the rime in the second line, but might be satiated by its repetition in the third; and so that line is left blank. Then the recurrence of the rime in the fourth line comes like a pleasant memory, and moreover pleases by contrast with the blank one.

The elder children should certainly be helped to appreciate the artistic beauty of some of the more intricate stanza-forms; the study of the structure of Matthew Arnold's 'Scholar Gipsy' and 'Thyrsis' stanza, for example, reveals in the architecture alone the genius of a great artist:—'Lament for Thyrsis':

a 5 Well! wind-dispersed and vain the words will be,
b 5 Yet, Thyrsis, let me give my grief its hour
c 5 In the old haunt, and find our tree-topp'd hill!
b 5 Who, if not I, for questing here hath power?
c 5 I know the wood which hides the daffodil,
a 3 I know the Fyfield tree,
d 5 I know what white, what purple, fritillaries
e 5 The grassy harvest of the river-fields,
e 5 Above by Eynsham, down by Sandford, yields,
d 5 And what sedged brooks are Thames's tributaries.

For more than a third of the way there is no rime; the music depends, as in blank verse, on the rhythm and cadence of the words: only a master's hand could dare so much; then just at the point when the ear is *almost* content to resign itself solely to the beauty of blank verse, but before it has quite ceased to listen for a rime, one comes: like the first bell that begins a chime; then one after another they chime in, and in the last quatrain they are ringing close and crowded in a full peal.

It was exactly the same artistic restraint that made Magdalen Tower one of the most beautiful buildings of the Middle Ages; in its lower stages there is no ornament; its beauty here is simply the beauty of perfect proportion, and of massive strength, fit support for its load; but above, in the belfry story, comes course upon course of ornamentation, till in parapet and pinnacles every stone is a carven jewel.[1]

[1] I can enjoy bread and cheese, and know nothing of gastronomy; but I believe that skilled culinary professors have arts to excite the

The order in which the long-looked-for rimes occur should be noted: the first of them, in the fourth line, echoes the second; the fifth, the third. And then, after long expectation comes the rime of the first line and completes the sestet. The interval is too long for any but a cultivated ear, but to an ear that has listened for the rime the pleasure is proportionate to the waiting. No other poet, I think, has used a stanza with rimes so far apart; the shortening of the sixth line lessens the interval and, more important, makes the stress on the last rime heavier. But it has also a further artistic significance: the reflective, even mournful, mood of the two poems needs long, slow lines for its expression, and so nine of the ten lines have five 'beats'. But a long stanza of such lines would tire the ear, and so the short line of only three 'beats' is introduced to give relief. Further it 'completes' the first set of rimes, the sestet, and so provides a natural pause, a kind of stanza-caesura; which divides, as a caesura should, unequally, so that the break comes after five lines and before four.

This Arnold stanza seems to me the most beautiful ever devised, and I have often wondered that so little has been written both of it and in it. If the Greeks, or Aristotle at least, were right in holding that a certain largeness is an essential element in a beautiful thing,[1] this stanza surely touches the limits of size possible in the unit of a poem—the sonnet of course is not a stanza but a complete whole in itself.

appetite by means of scraps and mouthfuls, keeping the stomach waiting and eager, to surfeit it with sweets at last.

[1] I believe that our modern Corinthians hold a similar view of the relative value of large and small animals.

Boys who are sufficiently advanced to appreciate the beauty of form in this stanza will find interest and critical training in a comparative study of stanza-forms, e.g. in comparing Spenser's form in the *Faery Queen* with Prior's modification of it:

It often falls in course of common life, *a*
That right long time is overborne of wrong *b*
Through avarice, or power, or guile, or strife, *a*
That weakens her and makes her party strong: *b*
But Justice, though her doom she doth prolong *b*
Yet at the last she will her own cause right *c*
As by sad *Belge* seems, whose wrongs though long *b*
She suffered, yet at length she did requite *c*
And sent redress thereof by this brave Briton knight, *c*

and

To the close rock the frighted raven flies *a*
Soon as the rising eagle cuts the air, *b*
The shaggy wolf unseen and trembling lies *a*
When the hoarse roar proclaims the lion near. *b*
Ill-starred did we our forts and lines forsake *c*
To dare our British foes to open fight, *d*
Our conquest we by stratagem should make, *c*
Our triumph had been founded upon flight. *d*
'Tis ours by craft and by surprise to gain, *e*
'Tis theirs to meet in arms and battle on the plain. *e*

To Johnson's ear Prior's stanza had lost none of the power of pleasing in throwing overboard Spenser's intricate and difficult repetition of rimes. But we know from his criticism of 'Lycidas', that good as his ear was for balance and rhythm and the harmony of prose, he could never appreciate the finer music of poetry. To prefer Prior's stanza to Spenser's is to prefer a chime on four bells to the Magdalen peal; for indeed it is not properly a stanza but simply two quatrains of four lines completed by a couplet; there is no common rime to link together the parts and give unity to the whole.

I have often used these stanzas as a test of musical appreciation, and I have found that three out of four boys prefer the Spenser form when they read them to themselves, and nine out of ten, at least, when the stanzas are recited or read to them.

The difference between them is exactly the same in kind as the difference between the Miltonic and Shakespearian sonnet-forms, though it is less in degree. The almost immeasurably superior musical capacity of the older form is often unappreciated because the supreme genius of Shakespeare was able to draw such music from the inferior instrument as hardly any one else could produce from the better one. But there is perhaps no more striking evidence of their respective merits than that there *were* other men, e. g. Milton, Wordsworth, Keats, and even Rossetti, whose best sonnets can bear comparison with Shakespeare's. In all else he stands alone, but as a sonnet-writer he has his peers. When Ben Jonson said he 'wanted art' he was not thinking of his sonnets, but I believe that in them, if anywhere, the statement may be justified. I often wonder, what 'The Expense of Spirit', the most powerful, but not the finest, sonnet in the language, would have been if its power had concentrated in and expressed itself through the finer medium of the Petrarchan form. But this is perhaps going beyond the scope of elementary criticism.

Another fascinating study is to attempt to trace correspondence between the spirit of a poem and its stanza-form to see how the soul informs the body. Every one, I suppose, must realize that such a correspondence exists, that 'In Memoriam', for example, would have a different *meaning* if its stanza-*form* were different; but why this should be is very hard to explain.

I think that in Rabbi Ben Ezra, with its two short lines followed by the long rush of the third, I see a visible image of the poet's process of thought brooding over a deep and difficult subject—thoughts coming, as Shakespeare says of the words of a stammering speaker, like water out of a narrow-necked bottle, now in trickles now in gushes—

> Grow old along with me;
> The best is yet to be,
> The last of life for which the first was made.
> Our times are in His hand
> Who saith 'A whole I planned,
> Youth shows but half; trust God: see all nor be afraid.'

I have discussed stanza-form at some length, because, though it too often escapes study in school, it is a sort of test of literary appreciation. The art in it is quite unnoticed by an illiterate reader, but it is absolutely fundamental: literature is *form*; there are no literary *subjects*. From him who cannot receive this the meaning of art is hidden.

CHAPTER VI

PICTURES IN POETRY

> And as the imagination bodies forth
> The forms of things unknown, the poet's pen
> Turns them to shapes, and gives to airy nothing
> A local habitation and a name.

As the poet speaks in music which goes straight to the heart without translation by the intellect, so he speaks in pictures rather than in symbols—he gives us the thing itself and not its intellectual sign. Coleridge will not, or cannot, say simply 'in winter'; he must express himself by a picture and *show* us the time: it is

> When the ivy-tod is heavy with snow,
> And the owlet whoops to the wolf below
> That eats the she-wolf's young.[1]

Shakespeare will not say 'three years ago'; he shows us a pageant of the seasons,

> Three winters cold
> Have from the forests shook three summers' pride,
> Three beauteous springs to yellow autumn turn'd,
> Three April perfumes in three hot Junes burn'd
> Since first I saw you.

Instead of saying 'in the autumn' he calls up the spirit of the ruined year,

> When yellow leaves, or none, or few do hang
> Upon those boughs which shake against the cold,
> Bare, ruined choirs, where late the sweet birds sang,

[1] It should be noticed, in view of what comes later, that in this picture there are the *essentials* of winter: famished hunger, heavy snow, and the most characteristic sound; cf. 'When Icicles hang by the Wall'.

and in the next lines, instead of saying 'evening' and leaving us to imagine it for ourselves, he shows us sunset, twilight, and the dark as *his* glorious imagination saw them. One often hears 'practical' persons, whose childhood has been soured by paraphrasing and grammatical disquisitions, object to poets that 'they do not say plainly what they mean; if he means "it is three years since I saw you", why can't he say so simply *in plain prose*?' Now the way to help such people, if they have any intellectual interests at all (if they have not, as often happens, the case is hopeless), is to confront them with a piece of good prose, say a paragraph of Kingsley's scene on a tropical river in *Westward Ho*; or any one of a score of descriptive passages in Macaulay's[1] third chapter, e.g. of London streets, of border peels, of a typical highway; or Dickens's 'Yarmouth Beach' or what Rebecca saw from the window, in *Ivanhoe*—I take the first examples that come to mind. If the patient admits that these are good, or any of them, then he will be forced to agree that it is because they 'body forth the forms of things unknown' and make them real, and present to us so that we actually see them—in a word, because they speak to us in pictures. In what else lies the charm of the great novelists, of Fielding, whose pictures of country inns make wayfaring life in the eighteenth century more real to us than the morning's paper can make the events of yesterday, of Smollett, whose frigates we know better than Lord Fisher's newly-invented torpedo-proof batteries, of Scott, whose Monkbarns would more please than surprise us if he stopped us in the street to-morrow to inquire for the ruins of

[1] For such people are commonly radicals.

Rewley? Again, it is the master-secret of the great historians, from the Anglo-Saxon chroniclers downwards—I speak, unfortunately, as one who knows not Herodotus. Pater may take too limited a view when he declares that the only 'true business of the historian is to bring us face to face with energetic personalities', but it is certain that we can have no 'philosophy teaching by examples' from the past until we have been helped to appreciate its *reality*, to visualize its men and conditions as we do those of to-day. The historians who help us most are those who are most pictorial, i. e. those who are most poetical; those who say not 'in proportion as the manners, customs, and amusements of a nation are cruel and barbarous, the regulation of their penal codes will be severe', but 'when men delight in battles, bull-fights, and the combats of gladiators, they will punish by hanging, burning, and crucifying'. The men who have done most in our day to call up spirits from the vasty deep of time, and make them move and speak before us, have written in pictures, like poets; two of them who wrote *Puck of Pook's Hill* and *Richard Yea and Nay* are known as poets; another is Mr. C. R. L. Fletcher, whose *Introductory History of England* is as full of life and colour as a pageant.

Even in science, which is popularly supposed to be the antithesis of poetry, and to which the plain and practical men attach so much more importance, the greatest writers are those who present scientific facts in pictures. Mr. H. G. Wells has such poetical power to make facts seem as real as fiction that few will admit him to be a scientific writer. But the writings of Huxley, Grant Allen, Belt, Bates, Buckland, and Wallace, for example, are full of pictures; you can hardly open a page at random without coming upon facts pictorially presented. Even Darwin, for all his professed dislike of poetry, and its indubitably evil results on his style, is most successful in making his meaning clear when he gives it as in a picture. For instance, in chapter xii of the *Origin of Species* he is explaining the means by which species become distributed over the earth, and he gives us as an example:

'I suspended a duck's feet, which might represent those of a bird sleeping in a natural pond, in an aquarium where many ova of fresh-water shells were hatching; and I found that numbers of the extremely minute and just-hatched shells crawled on the feet and clung to them so firmly that when taken out of the water they could not be jarred off. These just-hatched molluscs survived on the duck's feet in damp air, from twelve to twenty hours; and in this length of time a duck or heron might fly at least six or seven hundred miles and would be sure to alight in a pool or rivulet if blown across sea to an oceanic island or to any other distant point.'

If he had always written like that the popular ideas of his 'theories' would be less ridiculous.

The structure of a horse's teeth is a highly scientific matter; but Huxley, by using the characteristic arts of poetry, makes it perfectly clear to every reader:

'The teeth of a horse are not less peculiar than its limbs. *The living engine, like all others, must be well stoked* if it is to do its work; and the horse, if it is to *make good its wear and tear*, and to exert the enormous amount of force required for its propulsion, must be well and rapidly fed. To this end good *cutting instruments* and powerful and lasting *crushers* are needful. Accordingly the twelve cutting teeth of a horse are *close-set and concentrated* in the fore part of its mouth, *like so many adzes or chisels.* The *grinders* or molars are large and have an extremely complicated structure, being composed of a number of different substances of unequal hardness. The consequence of this is that they wear away at different rates, and hence *the surface of each grinder is always as uneven as that of a good millstone.*

If the practical man is not yet convinced that the poet's method of telling things in pictures is the plainest of all possible ways of speaking, let us ask him : in what book of geology are the effects of the great secular changes in the earth's crust made so plain to us as in Tennyson's pictures ?

> There rolls the deep where grew the tree—
> Oh, earth, what changes hast thou seen ;
> There, where the long street roars hath been
> The stillness of the central sea.
>
> The hills are shadows and they flow
> From form to form, and nothing stands ;
> They melt like mists, the solid lands,
> Like clouds they shape themselves and go.

What botanist can tell us as much about pollen in a paragraph as the poet's 'fruitful cloud and living smoke', or what chemist can bring home to us the very *essence* of chemistry like

> From his ashes shall be made
> The violet of his native land?

So far from being obscure, the poet is the physician who saves us from 'that first distemper of learning, when men study words and not things'.

We ought to work and pray for the conversion of the

practical man, because he is a very important person in the schools. He exists, e. g., in the form of Mr. Holmes's older unregenerate inspectors who, having had a hard time themselves and won their promotion by certificates, are naturally convinced that learning is a necessary drudgery whose purpose is to help one on in the world; they do not suppose that boys can *like* poetry any more than they themselves do, but they insist on so many 'annotated' lines being got by heart, 'because the Board prescribes it'. I once suggested that poetry forcibly administered had the rather negative merits of Mrs. Squeers's brimstone and treacle, 'it came cheap and spoilt the boys' appetites', so that when they left school they would want no more of it. The inspector seemed to think that very natural and probable, but he reminded me that what they did when they left school was not my business!

Then the local authorities which now control the schools consist very largely of people who pride themselves on being 'business men'. There is no real opposition between business and poetry—else how should a nation of shopkeepers have produced the most and the greatest poets? but business men are apt to think more of the need of 'a' living than of living when you have it; and as they see that poetry has no relation to the one they do not consider it in relation to the other.

Last and most important, the parents of primary school children, wise as most of them are—much wiser than the so-called 'lower middle class', for they realize better that life is more than meat and the body than raiment—tend to regard poetry as a mere 'accomplishment'. They like to hear 'Our Bill' recite 'The Boy stood on the Burning Deck', but they do not appreciate (how should they?) the importance of poetry to the life of the mind. . . .

'Art is imitation', and poetry is the supreme art because it gives us not only sound, like music, and form, like sculpture, and colour, like painting, but unites them all, and affects the senses like reality itself. Indeed we might even say that the images of poetry are more real than reality: what we see with the eye is outside us, objective; but 'when Shakespeare describes a thing you more than see it: you *feel* it too'—you feel it, i.e. 'inside' as children say. We can look, e.g., at the snowy roofs and fields of a winter landscape with no sense of cold, if we are well clad and healthy; but we cannot hear or read

> Deep on the convent-roof the snows
> Are sparkling to the moon:
> My breath to heaven like vapour goes!
> May my soul follow soon! . . .

without feeling the presence of a frost that has frozen everything into absolute stillness and silence: the cold is inside us.

The pictures in poetry are first ideal images—of

> Magic casements, opening on the foam
> Of perilous seas, in faery lands forlorn

of

> Sandstrewn caverns, cool and deep,
> Where the winds are all asleep,
> Where the spent lights quiver and gleam,
> Where the salt weed sways in the stream,
> Where the sea-beasts ranged all round,
> Feed in the ooze of their pasture ground,
> Where the sea-snakes coil and twine,
> Dry their mail and bask in the brine . . .

of

> Flowers azure, black and streaked with gold,
> Fairer than any waking eyes behold,

of

> Old palaces and towers
> Glittering within the waves' intenser ray,
> All overgrown with azure moss, and flowers
> So sweet the sense faints picturing them,

and secondly, clear and faithful presentations of observed and observable fact—of flowers:

> The rathe primrose that forsaken dies,
> The tufted crow-toe and pale jessamine,
> The white pink and the pansy freaked with jet,
> The glowing violet.
> The musk-rose and the well-attired woodbine
> With cowslips wan, that hang the pensive head,
> And every flower that sad embroidery wears,

and

> Gold-dusted snapdragon,
> Sweet-william with his homely cottage smell,
> And stocks in fragrant blow,
> Roses that down the alleys shine afar,
> And open, jasmine-muffled lattices,
> And groups under the dreaming garden trees,
> And the full moon and the white evening star,

of cities, like our own:

> Sweet city with her dreaming spires,
> She needs not June for beauty's heightening,

and London:

> The city now doth like a garment wear
> The beauty of the morning; silent bare,
> Ships, towers, domes, theatres, and temples lie
> Open unto the fields and to the sky
> All bright and glittering in the smokeless air

and hills, and the sea, and ships, and things in the sky above and in the earth beneath ; for all the kingdoms of the world and the glory of them are the poet's province.

It is ours to reveal to children the delight of finding and appreciating these beauties of description ; and ours to study with them the art by which they are created. The essential attribute of that art is its absolute precision, due first to a definiteness of vision clear as his who 'was in the spirit on the Lord's day', secondly to an intuitive perception of *essential* characteristics, and thirdly to an equally instinctive sense of the one and only word. All these are *gifts*, incommunicable, inexplicable; all that education can give a poet is experience and a vocabulary. With these gifts a poet can never be vague, and without them he can never be vivid.

The last gift is the only one that criticism can examine, the others we can only know by their consequences; but into the master-secret of the epithet we *can* learn to penetrate, and we shall find it to lie in the choice of words into which the most ideas are concentrated—for condensation is one of the unfailing marks of poetry [1]—words that crystallize a perfect description into a single phrase or adjective, that seize upon the most vital characteristic of the thing described, its essence, words vibrating with life, movement, and colour, that thrill the senses with their sheer *physical* appeal.

A poet stands on a high cliff and looks down on the sea below ; it moves, it murmurs, it heaves, it ebbs and

[1] And the greatest is the most highly concentrated, vide criticism of some lines of 'Lycidas' in *Sesame and Lilies*. A *mechanical* touchstone for poetry would be the trial to express precisely the same ideas in fewer words : all good poetry would baffle the attempt.

flows, it shimmers, it glitters, it has waves and troughs made tiny by the immense height—what among all this are its *typical* traits by which we may know it, and in what words is the perfect expression of them? Tennyson answers with two words, each as common as life and death:

> The *wrinkled* sea beneath him *crawls.*

That is final. So long as language lasts and men have eyes, that picture of the sea from above remains for men to approve. Aubrey Beardsley could work a miracle with a very few strokes of a pencil; but not with two.

The same poet stands beside other water, not bright and moving, but dark, sullen, deep, and still, those cold, forbidding *mysterious* depths that contrast so strangely with the smiling, dancing, broken water below the mill. What words will he choose to fix for ever the essential things in this picture?

> A sluice with *blackened* waters *slept.*

It is impossible to paraphrase that; there is more in the epithet 'blackened' than colour, depth, mystery, an eerie feeling: there is something beyond explanation, which in painting is called atmosphere, a thing to be *felt*, not talked about. There is 'all the charm of all the Muses, flowering in a lonely word'.

Such words as these are the 'inevitable' or as Professor Saintsbury calls them the 'absolute' words: once used they are felt to be final, of the very nature of things; no other words will do. They are perhaps, more than any other, the mark of genius, for to explain their genesis baffles criticism. It is not a question of keen observation and a good vocabulary, for the facts observed are obvious to all and the words are common to all; it is the instinctive selection of fundamentals among all the facts observed and of the precise words out of the whole vocabulary. This throws us back on the hypothesis of inspiration. We may follow the *art* of Gray or FitzGerald through version after version to the final polished product; but even if we did not know that Shakespeare 'never blotted a line' we feel that his pictures—of

> 'The *burning crest*
> Of the *old feeble* and *day-wearied* sun'

> 'Of *moving accidents* by *flood* and *field*
> Of *hair-breadth* 'scapes i' the *imminent deadly* breach
> Of being taken by the *insolent* foe . .'

> 'Of antres *vast* and desarts *idle*'

of forlorn virgins

> Chanting *faint* hymns to the *cold fruitless* moon

of stars still

> *Quiring* to the *young-eyed* cherubim

and a thousand such mysteries of perfect description came into being not by the pangs of human labour, but sprang like Athene from the head of Zeus. So with Keats, who wrote the 'Ode to a Nightingale' in a morning, we feel, as Mr. Stopford Brooke said, as if 'Nature herself had discovered the right word for him'. That is why Matthew Arnold classed him with Shakespeare.

Of Matthew Arnold himself it may be said that the happy epithet was his greatest gift. His favourite, 'shy', is a most beautiful and suggestive one, but he has used it perhaps too often—three times in the 'Scholar Gipsy', twice in successive stanzas, and once again in 'Thyrsis'.

One or two of them, however, must underlie the grave charge of inaccuracy: he was not always, like the great poets, a minute observer. Thus, the backs of the swallows that haunt the glittering Thames, are not black but steely blue; and the stalks of the corn grow yellow first at the root, so that he ought to have written

> Round *green stalks* and *yellowing roots* I see
> Pale blue convolvulus in tendrils creep.

It is in the use of epithets that the poet is most often a maker of language: his genius gives him both vision and the words to make others see. But he does not so much make new words as new uses, or what is practically the same thing, restore old uses; words tend to become conventionalized, narrow, and lifeless: poets give them back their early freshness, so that we feel some of the joy and wonder that early men must have had when language was in the making—'*surly*, *sullen* bell', '*blond* meadowsweet', '*faint sweet* cuckoo-flowers', '*thin* anemones', '*long dun* wolds, *ribbed* with snow'—these are all common words enough, so familiar that they have become almost contemptible and unpoetic; but it needed a poet's vision to see in them the quality that expresses the very essence of meadow-sweet or cuckoo-flowers or a tolling bell or the wind-swept flanks of the high wolds in winter.

This freshness, which is the life of the epigram, is never far from poetry, but very often we find a perfect description in ordinary words in their ordinary meanings:

> The last red leaf is whirled away.

The beauty in that depends not on any charm of freshness of phrase or meaning but purely on the consummate artistry which selects significant traits: the *last* leaf leaves the trees bare: that one word gives a whole background to the picture; *red* puts into it the single splash of vivid colour in a sombre canvas which in some famous pictures seems in some subtle way to modify the whole; *whirled* gives movement and life to the scene, it sets the trees swaying for us and carries the spot of colour across the face of the picture.

Colour in poetry is of great importance to children. We, as a nation, have not enough of it; there is probably more in Browning's pictures than in all the rest of our poets—which suggests the influence of the great Italian masters, among whose works he spent so much of his life. Keats often gives us rich colour, but there is generally something of Rembrandt in it, browns and old golds and purple shadows. The colour that pleases children is the clear bright varied hues of the open air, not the atmosphere of Madeline's chamber, but of

> Three ducks upon a pond,
> A green bank beyond,
> The blue sky of spring,
> White clouds on the wing——
> Oh, what a little thing
> To remember for years,
> To remember with tears.

It is not so much in words as in phrases that the poet leaves his mark on language; the words that Shakespeare coined or fixed may be known to the dictionary-makers, but his 'Jewels five words long' have enriched the speech of humanity for ever. Part of our lessons in criticism should deal not only with the fitness of the epithet but with the fineness of the phrase. Too many of us, I am afraid, get our phrases filtered for us through the newspapers—that is why they are so often misquoted and misapplied. Nine men out of ten who piously reflect that 'the Lord tempers the wind to the shorn lamb' imagine that they have biblical warrant for believing so, whereas the man who first gave extended currency to the phrase was, though a parson, as pagan a writer as ever lived.

To use another's phrase surely and well—and there is no greater help in writing—we ought to have won it, to have seen it in its place, appreciated it and picked it out for ourselves. Then it is legitimate spoil, as much ours as his who cast it.

I think that all children should learn at school to keep a commonplace book, if only for this purpose alone—just as an apprentice used gradually to accumulate his stock of tools. There will then be some hope that they will continue the habit when they leave us; there is no sound reading which relies on memory unaided—unless we were all Macaulays or Scotts. The hope may be faint, it must be faint, when boys leave school at fourteen to return to homes where books are few and bookish influences fewer. But if every elementary school succeeded in producing but one real lover of literature yearly, the money spent on education would be more than justified in succeeding generations.

Sometimes, when existing language is inadequate to express his vision, the poet does coin new words; Tennyson so gave us 'yellowing' bowers, a word for what had before required a phrase, Keats gave us 'palely' loitering, a pictorial adverb, Byron gave us 'dayless' gloom. But Keats's 'parle' of voices, Madeline 'all amort', and still more some of his hyphenated words remind us that part of the training in criticism is the careful scrutiny of new coinage, for in it lurks a danger both for poets and their disciples. Making new words, by combining old ones particularly, is so easy and fascinating that there is a temptation to use them even when the old currency is fully adequate; Tennyson's early poems are full of them —rose-lips, silk-soft, faint-blue, sand-erased, sabbath-drawler, and bright-eyed, wild-eyed, and hawk-eyes, all in one short poem. Most of us have been intoxicated in youth by their fascination; one gets a delightful feeling of writing poetically in making single-word pictures by hyphenating the noun and its epithet. Yet nothing better illustrates the progress of Tennyson's art than his gradual disuse of the practice; for *restraint* is the mark of the supreme artist's work, and it is because the young Keats died before he had had time to develop it, that we are still uncertain whether his was a supreme genius or not.

In this attribute more than in Walter Bagehot's 'choice of subject' we shall find the secret of that quality which we call 'classic', both in architecture and poetry. Lack of it has been the ruin of art again and again; it marred the Greek orders in Roman hands, and utterly debased them in English; it was one of the chief causes of Gothic deterioration; and though Shakespeare, like a god, was a law unto himself, its effects within a few years of his death brought poetry in England lower than it has ever been since we have had a literature at all. For lawlessness is sweet in the flower but bitter indeed in the fruit.

I will quote as a warning to the young a sentence of Mr. Kipling's to illustrate how licence, so far from enriching language, may corrupt it with 'flash' coin: 'Between the snow-white cutter and the flat-topped honey-coloured rocks on the beach, the green water was troubled with shrimp-pink prisoners-of-war bathing'. That, with its clash of crude colours, is not a picture but a poster. But, unfortunately, like a Victorian oleograph, it appeals to untrained tastes, or rather to tastes perverted by the cheap journalism which infected us from America twenty years ago. That influence, almost universal in the homes from which our children come, is the worst enemy that we have to face in our English lessons—far worse than the vernacular of the home or the slang of the street, and so before we leave Mr. Kipling's sentence I will try to suggest how children may be helped to criticize his epithets.

In the first place two of them at least are ugly in sound, flat-topped, and shrimp-pink; the clash of the medial *t*'s and *p*'s and the repetition of *i*, the least musical of the vowels, help to explain why; then they are all crude and glaring, not rich and deep—if any one will read them side by side with the picture of the water-snakes in the 'Ancient Mariner', or of the flowers in Shelley's 'Dream of the Unknown', he will *feel* the difference; and only in snow-white, which indeed is not of Mr. Kipling's coinage, do the two elements in the compound *mutually beautify* each other. Shrimps, boiled of course, may modify pink, but not in the least beautify it, and honey only modifies colour very indefinitely. And vivid as the picture is, like the L. N. W. R. posters of Llandudno, it is only true in an impressionist sense: sea water is not green except in patches and those constantly changing, men's skins vary from white to brown and all of them are different in colour, shadows and reflections from the waves patch the whiteness of cutters. I am not competent to discuss the merits of the impressionist school in painting, but I know that great literature seizes on the permanence in things, and I believe too that great painting, unlike photography, catches something more than a phase, that the artist looks deeper than externals, and sees and fixes for us what Tennyson called 'a sense of the abiding in the transient'. What would a photographer have made of Dr. Johnson? Yet Reynolds saw and makes us see the man as he was, not merely his appearance; a face, for all his dim eyes and scrofulous skin, to study and delight in.

However, the final test for new words is not so much their intrinsic merit as their necessity: are the existing words inadequate to express the idea? Many of our new scientific words are deplorable in themselves, but their coinage is justified by the need of a new term to express a new notion.

No one knows better than Mr. Kipling that the resources of the English language had not been searched in vain when he wrote his unfortunate sentence in the American tongue.

At the risk of breaking the thread of the chapter, let me quote as a contrast to this a poem of Mr. Kipling's in English:

> They shut the road through the woods
> Seventy years ago;
> Weather and rain have undone it again,
> And now you would never know
> There was once a road through the woods
>   Before they planted the trees.

It is underneath the coppice and heath
  And the thin anemones;
  Only the keeper sees
That where the ringdove broods,
  And the badgers roll at ease,
There was once a road through the woods.

Yet if you enter the woods
  Of a summer evening, late,
    When the night-air cools on the trout-ringed pools
  Where the otter whistles his mate—
They fear not men in the woods
  Because they see so few—
    You will hear the beat of a horse's feet
And the swish of a skirt in the dew
Steadily cantering through
  The misty solitudes
As though they perfectly knew
  The old, lost road through the woods . . .
  But there is no road through the woods.

There Mr. Kipling is for once with the immortals: he has shown us a scene, not 'on any common earth', not 'in the light of common day', by which we perforce must see the workaday world, not in the flash and glare of an American searchlight, but a scene in Merlin's Isle of Gramarye in that light which never was on sea or land, but only in the poet's soul and in the country of his dreams.

We see the woods as clearly as we saw the shore, but we see them through an atmosphere that invests them with mystery: on the shore there was no presence but the sailors; but here we have a sense of something unseen, it is

A savage place, as holy and enchanted
As e'er beneath a waning moon was haunted
By woman wailing for her demon lover.

And we know that if we walked in that wood we should tread softly and speak low and look around us a little fearfully, like children. This means that a poet has put his spell upon us and is waking our imaginations to creative activity, independently of his own vision, by suggesting more than he shows us. I do not think Mr. Kipling's verse has anywhere else, not even in Puck's Song, so large an element of this suggestiveness that is inseparable from great art. Neither has he anywhere written sweeter music; the melody is largely due to the delicious echoes of his subtle rimes.

Lastly, it is a good exercise in criticism to compare the epithets in his picture of English woodland with those in his American poster:

'Weather and rain have *undone* it again,'
'*Thin* anemones,'
'The badgers *roll at ease*'—

common words all of them, yet it needed a poet's vision to see that each was the very word to express the essential thing. And by a happy chance he has given us a genuine new coin to compare with his own spurious metal, '*trout-ringed* pools', a word as beautiful in its sound as in its image; and a legitimate birth.

The artist's hand *must* be subdued to what it works in; he must be bound by the nature of his medium;[1]

[1] Reynolds, who knew nothing of glass, produced at New College something which is not a window, because it obscures the light, nor a fine picture, because glass is not a suitable medium for fine painting. The older artists who produced the other windows in the ante-chapel

and his triumph is not in defying its laws but in expressing himself gloriously within their limits. That is why the perfect sonnet is the most beautiful of all poems.

> Nuns fret not at their convent's narrow room,
> And hermits are contented with their cells,
> . . . Bees that soar for bloom
> Will murmur by the hour in foxglove bells:
> In truth the prison, unto which we doom
> Ourselves, no prison is.

It is only the feeble who claim 'poetic licence': great poets increase the resources of language less by coining new words than by revealing the full powers of old ones. For 'in tennis all play with the same ball: but one places it best'. We have seen how genius discerns and calls forth the latent poetic force of common epithets to show us pictures, but infinitely more important than this extension of literal meaning is the figurative use of language, which we have now to study.

have given us light and beautiful colour as well: they understood and accepted the nature of their medium.

CHAPTER VII

THE FIGURES OF SPEECH

Summer set lip to earth's bosom bare
And left the flushed print in a poppy there;
Like a yawn of fire from the grass it came,
And the light wind puffed it to flapping flame;
With burnt mouth, red like a lion's, it drank
The blood of the sun as he slaughtered sank,
And dipped its cup in the purpurate shine
When the eastern conduits ran with wine.

THE clearness of vision and the originality of mind which make a poet see the application of common words outside their conventional use—which make him, for example, see 'dun' in clouds and skies and woods and distant hills, while a dairyman sees it only in cows—which enable him to seize upon *typical* attributes, reveal to him also the identity of attributes in diverse things so that he is able to give us a picture of one thing by using the epithets, or even the very name, of another.

So Ben Jonson, wishing to give us the image of a lady, and finding the common words that describe others cannot express her charms, looks round him to see where each is found in most perfection and bids us look there for her likeness:

Hast thou seen but a white lily grow
  Before rude hands have touched it?
Hast thou marked the fall of snow
  Before the soil hath smutched it?

Hast thou felt the fur of the beaver,
Or swans down ever?
  Or hast smelt the smell o' the brier,
  Or the nard in the fire?
  Or hast tasted the bag o' the bee?
O so white, O so soft, O so sweet is she

It is as if a painter could dip his brush into the rose itself and transfer its living blush to his pallette—it is more, for similes can speak to every sense; not only

My love is like a red, red rose
That 's newly sprung in June;

but

My love is like the melody
That 's sweetly played in tune.

So to Blake, feeling himself and wishing to make us feel the insatiate fierceness, cruelty, energy, and splendour which are the essence of the tiger's nature, comes the revelation that all these are the essential attributes of fire also; he can, if he chooses, compress them all into a single simile; but he does more, he concentrates them in one marvellous metaphor,

Tiger, tiger, *burning* bright,

probably the finest single word in all literature. Or Shakespeare, to paint the sadness and desolation of trees from which the summer glory has departed with its music of bird-song and richness of apparel, calls up another picture, that must have awakened in his day an even more poignant feeling than now, of desecrated churches, rifled of their vestments, their organs silent and their singers scattered, windowless, roofless and open to the winter sky, solitary and fast crumbling to decay. All these ideas and the *atmosphere* or *feeling* accompanying them he transfers to the trees condensed into three short words

> *Bare, ruined choirs,* where late the sweet birds sang.

But, as in the deepest depth a lower depth is found, so sometimes the highest degree in which an attribute exists will not satisfy the poet as a comparison, and then he resorts to hyperbole—

> They were swifter than eagles; they were stronger than lions;

or that wonderful hyperbole by which Tennyson expresses the deathless power of love:

> My dust would hear her and beat
> Had I lain for a century dead,
> Would start and tremble under her feet
> And blossom in purple and red.

Again by the device—I ought rather to say by his instinct, of investing inanimate nature with the attributes of human beings, by making persons of things, the poet makes his pictures more real than reality for us:

> They rowed her in across the *hungry* foam,
> The *cruel, crawling* foam—

no sea that physical eyes have seen could make us shudder as that figure does.

These four pictorial figures of speech, particularly metaphor the greatest of them, are to poetry what a colour box is to painting. Some understanding of them is fundamental to any intelligent study of literature, and nothing in language-teaching is more important than helping children to an appreciation of their value. Through them mainly poetry achieves that concentration which is one of the marks of all great art; they are the principal medium by which the vision of the poet's mind flashes upon our own, and the great miracle of genius is wrought 'that things which are not should be as though they were, that the imaginations of one mind should become the personal recollections of another'.

I have sometimes wondered whether their Greek or Latin names are a sort of bugbear in teaching, but there is really no difficulty here at all. The *things* are no more Greek than physicians or pedagogues—and their ways are less incomprehensible to children. They are a kind of picture-writing such as early people had before they learned, or could learn, without the concrete and the visual. And they illustrate again my point that poetry is a *natural* study of childhood. Of children's instinctive power to *use* the figures no less than to appreciate them I shall speak in a separate chapter.

Simile is the simplest of the figures, and I suppose philologists would tell us it is the oldest; the easiest way to give an idea of an unknown thing, e. g. a tiger, is to say it 'is like' a known thing, viz. a cat; such an elementary form of simile is used and understood by babies. But in poetry it is usually a single attribute, rather than a group, that the writer seeks to present; then he thinks of a thing which possesses that attribute in the highest degree and calls up its image into the reader's mind so that he may 'abstract' its attribute and transfer it to the image of the thing described. Thus Tennyson, to give us an idea of the dark eyelashes of a girl we can only see through his vision, remembers that the one place in the world where their shade can be matched is in the buds of the ash in late spring, and tells us they were

Black as ashbuds in the front of March.

Of this beautiful simile we must notice two things—to help us and to warn. It is not any mere *blackness* that Tennyson is seeking; it is that blackness, soft yet brilliant, a kind of bloom, which is found only in beautiful hair and in the ashbuds in spring; and secondly, a simile must introduce no jarring secondary idea, its attribute must be, not pure which is impossible, but so dominant that its other qualities never occur to the mind; thus 'black as soot' or even 'coal', apart from their failure to express the exact shade, would have been defective because the secondary idea of grime and even baseness could not be prevented from intruding into the mind, blurring and spoiling the picture. This does not mean that no secondary idea at all should accompany the image, but that no jarring *pictorial* element should intrude itself: often a fine simile pleases both eye and ear; Tennyson, for example, uses a simile to give a picture of a man with

> Arms on which the standing muscles sloped
> As slopes a wild brook o'er a little stone,
> Running too vehemently to break upon it.

Here the extraordinary correspondence between the swiftness and sound of the brook and the movement and music of the words in the last line compels our notice, but rather heightens than detracts from our pleasure in the picture.

The perfect simile, as Johnson said, 'must both illustrate and ennoble the subject; must show it to the understanding in a clearer view and display it to the fancy with greater dignity'. Thus Butler's

> Like a lobster boiled, the morn
> From black to red began to turn,

compares the greater to the less, the fine thing to the mean one, and so, in spite of its wit, it offends a sensitive taste. And on the other hand, Byron's comparison of a rainbow above a torrent to

> Love watching madness with unalterable mien,

though it sounds dignified and grand, does not put anything 'in a clearer view'; it is mere meaningless bombast. So many of Shelley's similes in the 'Skylark'—'like a high-born maiden', 'like a rose', 'like a glowworm'—do not make the bird more real, but less real to us; they take our attention away from its song to fix it upon irrelevant pictures.

I have spoken of concentration as an essential attribute of the highest poetry; the finest figure, like the finest epithet, is that into which the most ideas are condensed: in 'High Tide' two similes occur together to illustrate this point. We are shown a picture of the tidal wave,

> It swept with thunderous noises loud,
> Shaped *like a curling snow-white cloud,*
> Or *like a demon in a shroud.*

Here the second simile is infinitely finer than the first, because there is far more involved in it: a cloud is simply a shape, and a vague one; but a demon is a thing of fear and force and malice and mischief; more, it is a personal thing and so more real; and most of all and above all a shrouded demon is a *mysterious* thing; mystery, a sense of some presence not of this world, is an essential element in poetry.

Poetry is so full of similes that there can be little

excuse for quoting more—except the pleasure of recalling them for the purpose. Chaucer's

> Reed as the bristles of a sowès ear,

which is the finest touch in the miller's portrait, reminds us of the single simile which, among all the subtle touches that go to make the portrait we know best in Shakespeare, is the most telling and significant: it shows us Falstaff walking before his page

> Like a sow that has overwhelmed all her litter but one.

Shelley's 'Skylark' and Byron's 'Sennacherib' are all simile—but

> Like as the waves make towards the pebbled shore,
> So do our minutes hasten to their end. . . .

Metaphor is by far the most important, as it is the commonest, figure of speech. In its origin every metaphor is poetry, an attempt to express an emotion within by an image or picture of something external; thus my 'explanation' is 'laying out flat' the ideas 'involved', i. e. 'rolled up' in the term. But thousands of metaphors have been household words so long that they have acquired a direct and literal meaning; they are 'fossil-poetry' and are used with no consciousness of their difference from other words, as coal is used without remembrance of its former life in sun and rain and wind. Some metaphors again, like 'stand up for', 'grounds for belief', &c., are in the peat stage, dead but not yet fossilized; they have become commonplace and no longer stir the faintest thrill of emotion, but in using them we are still conscious that they are figures of speech.

But though we rightly and necessarily use dead metaphors as ordinary words, we only do so with full intelligence when their metaphorical meaning is in our subconsciousness; no one, for example, can completely understand the word 'metaphor' unless he knows, or has known, that it was originally used in a *physical* sense to express a 'carrying across' of something. It is therefore of great importance to the language-lessons that the children should have etymological dictionaries and that they should form the habit of looking *always* for a metaphor that may be fossilized in the word they turn up.[1]

However, we are most concerned here with living figure of speech, the metaphor that awakens in us the emotion that brought it into being. For these figures, let me repeat, *are* the products of an emotional state; the companions in arms of Richard I were not stating simply their *conception* that he was a brave man when they called him Cœur de Lion: they were trying to express the *feeling* that his valour stirred in them, to say not what they *thought*, but what they *felt* about him. To an excited imagination he ceased to be a man and became a symbol, all his other attributes sinking out of sight, and they gave him the name of the symbol of warlike prowess and called him the lion's heart. This is the essence of a metaphor, that a thing is visualized as the symbol of an attribute.

A simile is always a phrase, a metaphor usually a word; but it is a mistake to regard their difference merely as one of form; the real difference is in the degree of imaginative stimulus. 'He fought like a lion' is a weaker

[1] Incidentally it follows that no one can use the full range of English with a sure hand who has not been well grounded in the ancient tongues.

image than 'He was a lion in the fight', because it involves two distinct pictures; one must

> Look now upon this picture, now on that,

whereas the metaphor fuses man and lion into one idea.

Children usually have no difficulty in *recognizing* a metaphor and interpreting the primary picture in it: but in a fine metaphor so many images are concentrated that they need help in appreciating its full force and beauty. For example, if children are reading Blake's 'Little Black Boy' and come to the metaphor

> This black body and this sunburnt face
> Are but a *cloud* . . .

they will readily see that the body is pictured as a cloud, because in a body of cloud you cannot see clearly; but they will not so readily appreciate a cloud as the symbol of *partial* obscurity, though it hides the source of warmth and light, yet it allows them to reach us; nor will they notice without help that the cloud is essentially transitory, it is the symbol of the evanescent; again, that deeper suggestion that only by the death of the material part of us can we know God is fundamental to the metaphor, but will not be perceived by the child unaided. Yet all these ideas, at least, are *in* the figure and must be revealed before children can fully appreciate it.

So when Wordsworth calls the daisy 'a nun', children must be helped to see in a nun the picture of modesty, shyness, gentleness and purity made visible by means of a metaphor of three letters.

Any one who would appreciate the wealth of imagery concentrated in a fine metaphor should read, or read again, what Ruskin found in Milton's 'blind mouths' in 'Lycidas'—more than two pages of *Sesame and Lilies*, i. 22.

The metaphors that present most difficulty are not those that 'call one thing by the name of another to give a better picture of it' (which I have found to be for children a sufficiently good description of most metaphors), but those derived from verbs—like Blake's 'burning'.

But the difficulty is less in appreciating them than in making and using them, and it was probably this kind of metaphor that Aristotle had in mind when he said that 'the greatest of all excellence is to be happy in the use of metaphor, for this alone cannot be acquired . . . and is a certain mark of genius'. However, a boy whom I have no reason to suspect either of genius or of plagiarism lately wrote in some original verse that

> The chestnut trees are *rusting* fast,

and I took some trouble to discover the genesis of the metaphor. The boy only remembered that the tree had reminded him of old, rusted machinery (i. e. he had seen a *typical* characteristic common to the two images, but most striking in the iron), and that he had tried to make a simile, but could not fit it to his metre. He must then, I suppose, have visualized not the *thing*, the machinery, but the action, and so got his picture 'rusting'. So Blake may perhaps have thought first of the tiger as a consuming fire and from that got a still higher image of 'burning'.

This kind of metaphor is however rare: usually when the poetic mind seeks to visualize *action* it puts the *agent* also into the picture—

> *Autumn's fire burns* slow along the woods

so metaphor merges into personification.

I suggested that simile was probably the oldest figure of speech, but personification also must be as old as language; when we speak of these figures as 'art' we need always to remember that they were first instinctive, they came not by man taking thought, but spontaneously, from his feeling. And even now the perfect figure, though we admire it as art, seems not to be 'thought out' by the poet, but to 'occur' to him; it is not sought for, it is simply the description of the vision that is his inexplicable gift. There is a remarkable instance of this in the figure put into the mouth of Horatio,

> But look the morn in russet mantle clad
> Walks o'er the dew of yon high eastern hill.

Horatio was not the man to see a vision of the dawn as a person; conscious art would have made him speak soldierly words more befitting his part. But Shakespeare had to tell that dawn was breaking, and as the fact occurred to him in a picture he made Horatio describe what he himself saw. It is in just such touches as this, where some one speaks for a moment out of character, that we get glimpses of Shakespeare the man, that was behind and within Shakespeare the artist. He did not consciously impersonate things to make his picture of them more real to his audience, but he seems always to have thought in persons rather than in things. He scarcely ever refers to the sea, for example, except as a person

> 'The rude sea's enraged and foamy mouth.'

> 'As good to chide the waves as speak them fair.'

> 'I saw him beat the surges under him
> And ride upon their backs;'

earth to him has always a 'bosom' or 'veins' or 'bones' or 'entrails'; fire (in Lear) is a minister of vengeance that will come when called, yet (King John)

> There is no malice in this burning coal,
> The breath of heaven hath blown his spirit out
> And strewed repentant ashes on his head.

Sleep is nature's soft nurse, night is death's second self that seals up all in rest.

In all this Shakespeare is much more primitive than Spenser or Wordsworth; personification is an instinct of primitive man; he does not so much 'See God in clouds and hear him in the wind'—that is more literally true of Wordsworth—as see personality in all things; children do the same, but civilized men, though they still retain 'gender' in most languages, only feel personal communion with external things, when emotion for the moment sits in reason's seat. Shakespeare, among the innumerable personalities that composed his identity, had a primitive myth-making child of the race. In the use of personification Shelley and Blake are nearest to Shakespeare.

To Wordsworth too, 'Nature was a person, distinct from himself, and capable of being loved. He could brood on her character, her ways, her words, her life. Hence arose his minute and loving observation of her and his passionate description of all her charms.' But that is worlds away from primitive man and children and Shakespeare; it is a much more intellectual idea, as Shelley says of it, 'it is a sort of thought in sense'. Wordsworth sees all things as manifestations of one personality, not as individual persons: in him the myth-maker never altogether worked independently of the philosopher.

Spenser's personification represents a third type; he is more the conscious artist, like Collins and Tennyson; he has visions of things as persons, of course; but they are called up by him rather than come to him instinctively. He calls them because he delights in them; but also because he knows that by describing them he will make his pictures more real to his readers, will make them *felt* more. 'Man never knows how anthropomorphic he is': the most 'real' thing to him is that which is nearest himself, which has most of his own attributes; he is a social animal and instinctively seeks for communion with other beings; the same instinct which a child gratifies when she talks to her doll makes men find pleasure in imagining things as persons. In a word, it is our nature to take more *interest* in a personified thing. And that is why the poets use the figure, consciously or unconsciously, for their own delight or for ours.

The attributes of things are intensified by personification; the sea that drowns men is more terrible when conceived as a purposeful being than as a blind and lifeless force, for man, in spite of all man's inhumanity to man, instinctively looks to *persons* for sympathy and fellowship, and his spirit as well as his body is hurt by cruelty.

We know so little of our own nature that much of what is called psychology is but vague speculation and hypothesis. But the myth of the Earth-mother may have its root in one of the deepest instincts of humanity. Unless indeed Berkeley and the mystics are right, man is but a few fragments of the earth's substance held together in a temporary association by the same chemical forces that give shape to all matter, soon to return by the continued action of those forces into the great reservoir of the inorganic, and anon to be regrouped by them into other forms. Scott's Meg Merrilies was crazed, but Keats's who felt:

> Her brothers were the craggy hills,
> Her sisters larchen trees,

and regarded all natural phenomena as her great family, was simply a primitive being in whom intellectual illusions had not weakened intuitive perceptions.

At moments all of us have the same feeling: we lift up our eyes to the hills for help, or cry to the sea breaking on its desolate rocks or find comfort because

> Our tree yet crowns the hill.

Ruskin may call it a 'pathetic fallacy' that leads men to do these things, but still they do them, and are persuaded that they find help and healing.

I have spoken at some length of personification because I believe that an instinct so strong in children should be more considered in the schools. There is no figure which children use so naturally, so easily, and so effectively. A child will write an infinitely better essay on the Thames, or on Autumn, or even on coal or steam, if he is asked to think of his subject as a person, than if he sets about it in the grown-up way. But I shall illustrate this point presently.

Between personification and apostrophe, the imaging things as persons and addressing them as such, children need draw no line.

The other figures of speech, except hyberbole, of

which something must be said, are of much less importance ; the essence of them, as of the greater figures, is the aid given to the imagination by the use of the concrete and the visual to body forth the abstract and ideal, of the known thing to suggest the unknown, of the familiar for the remote. Thus, using the figure with the rather cumbrous title synecdoche, we pray for our daily bread, using the name of the most typical food instead of the indefinite general term ; or we speak—thank God there are signs that we may soon be ashamed to do so any more—of a workman as a 'hand': 'hardly entreated brother' indeed, that thy marred, misshapen, work-roughened hand should stand for the whole body and soul of thee.

So, by metonymy, we make the well-known image of a crown or a sceptre stand for the unfamiliar figure of the sovereign whose identity is securely hidden from most of his subjects by the illustrated newspapers ; or we say, pleasantly and pictorially, of a friend that he is fond of 'the bottle' instead of using that vague term so dear to intemperate teetotallers, 'the drink'. It is the method of Hogarth and all the great artists.

Hyperbole is to poetry what the harmless exaggeration, natural to children, is to their story-telling—which indeed is a form of poetry. They like to come upon examples of it, and to use it themselves ; but it seems too primitive for modern taste. Pegasus in these days is tightly reined. In Homer's hands, to judge from Longinus and the translators, the thing became a trumpet to stir men's souls,

> Fierce as he passed the lofty mountains nod,
> The forests shake, earth trembled as he trod,

he says of Neptune; and

> While scarce the skies her horrid head can bound,
> She stalks on earth,

of Discord, and of course he says it far more magnificently in the Greek.

Shakespeare too uses it constantly, sometimes consciously, for effect:

> The sky, it seems, would pour down stinking pitch,
> But that the sea, mounting to the welkin's cheek,
> Dashes the fire out.

There the effect of the figure must surely be as sublime as anything in Homer. But when he makes a rude sea-captain tell the Duke of Suffolk he is like

> Ambitious Sylla, overgorged
> With gobbets of thy mother's bleeding heart,

we think of his audience and of the dyer's hand.

Hyperbole is always in danger of descending into bombast, as we are often reminded in reading Shakespeare's contemporaries. But 'those hyperboles are the best' says Longinus, and he says the same thing of all the figures, 'which have not the appearance of being hyperboles at all'. No one notices the exaggeration in the lines from 'The Tempest' until the emotion excited by them has passed away and he examines the figure critically; but an obvious hyberbole, except perhaps in Marlowe where the whole atmosphere is 'hyberbolical', produces effects contrary to those for which it was designed.

Here perhaps is a suitable place to say something of artifice as distinct from art.

I have already entered a caveat lest I should be suspected of being one of those persons flayed—but that their skins are so thick—by Ruskin, 'who fancy that Art may be learned as book-keeping is'. Art depends on vision and the gift of tongues, and these can no more be acquired than physical beauty. But though artists are born, they are not born ready-made any more than Helen was born beautiful: they have to grow, and they have to learn like other men, and criticism of their fellows' work will help them in their own. Criticism, as I have been trying to show, can be learned, and leaving artists out of the question, must be learned by those who would really appreciate their work.

It is true that the very greatest poetry, in Shakespeare often, in Keats and Shelley sometimes, in Wordsworth now and again, in Tennyson once or twice, does seem to be the absolutely spontaneously perfect expression of a feeling, an inspired voice: the fact is one of the great arguments for God. But these are exceptions to the human rule; they are the *ideal* poetry; and it is, partly, by studying them, that human powers learn to approach them. Human spontaneity alone, however, will not give us the highest poetry, without artistic form. Blake is the best example of this: he sings, as the linnet sings, absolutely without taking thought; but his poetry, with all the freshness of childhood, has childish faults of form which art could have smoothed away, if he had been more of an artist, without ceasing to be a seer. It is surely a pity that a charming and most characteristic little lyric like 'A Dream' should end in something that is neither a rime nor an assonance:

> Follow now the beetle's hum;
> Little wanderer, hie thee home,

when five minutes' revision would have found him a perfect rime.

The opposite extreme, which we find very often in Tennyson, Swinburne, and Matthew Arnold, pleases us even less, because it is *obviously* meant to please us more. Here the first, simple, spontaneous expression seems to have been so revised, smoothed, polished, and added to by *conscious* art, that though it has gained an artificial beauty it has lost a natural one.

Swinburne ends the first stanza of a poem that Blake might have begun, with the lines:

> Welling water's winsome word,
> Wind in warm, wan, weather.

Now Blake could never have written that; the power to do something like it was the one thing he lacked; but Swinburne had cultivated the power to too great a degree, and it has spoilt his stanza. The rest of it—'A Child's Laughter':

> All the bells of heaven may ring,
> All the birds of heaven may sing,
> All the wells on earth may spring,
> All the winds on earth may bring
> All sweet sounds together;
> Sweeter far than all things heard,
> Hand of harper, tone of bird,
> Sound of woods at sundown stirred—

is as fresh and natural as the voice of the birds, or the winds, or of Blake; but the last couplet is not art but artifice; it is beautiful, but it is made so by deliberate device, like the spots of white paint which Constable puts on his leaves and water to suggest reflection of lights.

The words are chosen for alliterative effect, and we can see it. Winsome is a beautiful word, but its use is a little, a very little, forced; and wan, also a beautiful word, with its atmosphere and its ethereal colour-sense is certainly out of harmony with warm.

In the best art we feel the effect without being conscious of the means used to produce it—sometimes indeed without being able, after all our study, to find them out.

Very often in Tennyson and Swinburne we can watch the hand of the conscious artist at work, 'loading every rift with gold', adding beauties till the simple texture of the original thought grows into stiff brocade. Their best work is not so wrought, but such work is more beautiful than the unpolished crystals of all but the greatest. Shakespeare or Blake or Shelley may cast from the crucible a flashing jewel that a single further touch could only spoil, but their temperature is their own secret; other men must cut and polish more or less, though the stone lose a little in glow while it gains in lustre. Better at least the polished gem than the shapeless stone which now gleams luridly and now is dull as glass, now glows like a carbuncle and now fades into a grey pebble.

But this would lead us into a discussion on Browning, which is far too big a matter for a little book like this. All I will say here is that beautiful form is the first essential of any work of art; pure gold or pure carbon are beautiful in themselves and in their nature; but until the artist's hand has shaped them, or until by some rare miracle he has *cast* them as perfect jewels, they are not art whatever else they may be.

CHAPTER VIII

OTHER ARTIFICES AND OTHER ARTS

True ease in writing comes from art not chance,
As those move easiest who have learned to dance.

THE power to thrill the heart with music and to light up the imagination with pictures belongs only to the poet's ear and eye; it is a gift. But besides their secret spell over the magic sound and the magic word poets and artists use, like ordinary people, various common devices that are at the disposal of us all.[1]

One of these is simple repetition of a word or phrase. As children say, and as pill-sellers know, 'you'll believe me if I say it twice'; and that seems to be human nature. Two of the most wonderful lines in the 'Ancient Mariner', as intensely charged with feeling as any in literature, are simply the repetition of three or four words—

Alone, alone, all, all, alone,
Alone on a wide, wide sea!

'Behold and see: is any sorrow like unto my sorrow?' By means of nine letters we are made to feel the climax of the mariner's punishment, and the depth of his despair, and a sense of utter solitude, and an illimitable waste of sea.

The two most fated persons of whom I have read are

[1] Even here, however, the poet often seems to do by instinct what ordinary writers do by design.

Richard II and Ravenswood, and each of them, in his bitterest hour, can find only a few words, and those repeated, to express his passion.[1] Richard cries for

> A little grave,
> A little, little, grave!

And Ravenswood, when Lucy returns the broken coin, can only repeat his wonder that she could have worn it next her heart while accepting his rival's addresses.

Lear's 'never' five times repeated is no human cry, and I at least can make no comment on it; but excepting that

> depth of some divine despair

I know no more poignant words than those Milton reiterates when for once his mighty self-control is overwhelmed by his grief at his cruel deprivation:

> Oh dark, dark, dark, amid the blaze of noon
> Irrecoverably dark, total eclipse
> Without all hope of day.

But here there is not only the repetition of the telling word and the reiteration of the idea: we are also made to feel the darkness by contrast with the blaze of noon.

This use of contrast, of which we have already noticed some examples, is one of the most effective artifices in all art; musicians and painters constantly employ it, and so do poets both in their pictures and in their music. Thus, in the 'Ancient Mariner', the terrible picture of the

[1] For only men incredulous of despair
Half-taught in anguish, through the midnight air,
Beat upward to God's throne in loud access
Of shrieking and reproach.

rotting deck, strewn with corpses with the death-dews on their limbs, is followed immediately by a scene of the most magical beauty, of moonlight on the waters and of the water-snakes at play. And this visual contrast is accompanied by a corresponding contrast in the music of the verse: the harsh, stern, aspirated stanza that tells:

> An orphan's curse would drag to hell
> A spirit from on high;
> But oh! more horrible than that
> Is a curse in a dead man's eye!
> Seven days, seven nights I saw that curse,
> And yet I could not die,

is succeeded by one of the most melodiously soothing stanzas in the whole poem:

> The moving moon went up the sky
> And nowhere did abide:
> Softly she was going up
> And a star or two beside.

So, by means of contrast, the great poet plays upon our emotions as the great musician on a violin.

Another fine example of the skilful use of this device is to be found in 'High Tide'. Elizabeth's husband comes riding up with might and main: we hear his voice raised in a great shout 'Elizabeth! Elizabeth!', and then comes the quiet parenthesis of the old mother:

> A sweeter woman ne'er drew breath
> Than my son's wife, Elizabeth.

I will not multiply examples, partly because any one who has once learned to look for them will find them everywhere in great art, and also because my last example reminds me of another artistic excellence which is, in a sense, the opposite of contrast, and which, for want of a special word, may be called consistency. The old mother's repetition of the words quoted is finely in keeping with her character as an *old* woman, and as a sweet and loving woman herself. It is but a little touch, but it is the touch of a true artist. One of the finest illustrations of this particular artistic merit is a poem of Dr. Bridges called 'Winter Nightfall'. It begins with a picture of a winter landscape at evening:

> The day begins to droop,—
>   Its course is done:
> But nothing tells the place
>   Of the setting sun.
>
> . . . .
>
> An engine pants and hums
>   In the farm hard by:
> Its lowering smoke is lost
>   In the lowering sky.
>
> The soaking branches drip,
>   And all night through
> The dropping will not cease
>   In the avenue.

Few stanzas that I know have such power as these to suggest the gloom of a rural landscape when the day and the year are alike ending: we are made to feel the palpable, damp, heavy atmosphere, and the heavy clouds seem to press upon our heads; moreover, the effect is progressive; the gloom deepens with each successive stanza; dark smoke is added to dark clouds, and the melancholy drone of a thresher and the equally monotonous drip of water saddens ear as well as eye. All this, however, is but to prepare us for a deeper gloom:

> A tall man there in the house,
> Must keep his chair;
> He knows he will never again
> Breathe the spring air;
>
> His heart is worn with work;
> He is giddy and sick
> If he rise to go as far
> As the nearest rick:
>
> He thinks of his morn of life,
> His hale, strong years,
> And braves as he may the night
> Of darkness and tears.

What is the gloom outside to the gloom in the house? And far deeper than any physical shadow is the gloomy hopelessness in the man's heart as he thinks of the darkness of the night into which he must go. What are lowering clouds and rain-drops to its darkness and tears?

Byron may have felt such a gloom, but Byron nowhere makes us feel it as these lines do. The sound of the poem, too, is marvellously in keeping with its sense; the slow monosyllables with their long vowels, the many pauses, owing to the short lines, make it sound, to me at least, like the dread formula heard from a deep voice in a hushed court at evening, when *one* must go forth and be no more seen.

The one well-planned novel of Dickens, *Great Expectations*, is curiously like Dr. Bridges' poem in maintaining one atmosphere throughout. It begins in fog on the marshland on a winter's afternoon, and the gloom that falls upon our spirits remains until the end—for of course Pip never really married Estella, it was foredoomed otherwise from the first; it deepens in Miss Havisham's darkened room, and in the bare blank brewery, and in the filthy associations of Smithfield Market and in the close, evil-smelling, murky atmosphere of the police-court; and it is in Pip's heart, and in our hearts, at the last.

'Winter Nightfall' in turn suggests by its use of the present tense, or as it has been called the historic present, another device of which Longinus says, 'when you introduce things past as actually present and doing, you will no longer relate, but display the very action before the eyes of your readers'. He gives an illustration from Xenophon, and, 'as every schoolboy knows', this is also Caesar's method. It is La Fontaine's too.

It is more common in prose than in poetry, for it is chiefly valuable in narrative, with which poetry has little to do. I mention it because I wish to suggest that children should be encouraged to use it, particularly in writing essays in history; it will demand that they should make pictures in their minds, have clear images of the things they are writing about—and, unless they do this, history is a barren and useless study.

From change of tense Longinus goes on to discuss change of person as a device 'powerfully effective, and oftentimes makes the hearer think himself actually present and concerned in the dangers described'; and he quotes Herodotus, 'You will sail upwards from the city Elephantina, and then you will arrive at a level coast. And when you have travelled over this tract of land you will go on board another ship and sail two days, and then you will arrive at a great city called Meroe.' And then he says, very justly, 'Do you see, my friend, how he carries your imagination along with him in his excursion: how he conducts you through the different scenes, converting hearing into sight? And all such passages, by appealing to the hearers personally, make them fancy themselves present in the actual transactions.' This device is the great secret of Mr. Belloc—or rather it is a part of his secret: the other and more important part is intimate personal acquaintance with the scenes of which he writes. He says '*You* will go to Jericho' because *he* has been to Jericho.

As in the last paragraph, I had an ulterior rather than a direct motive in referring to this device; but what that was will appear in the last chapter.

Here, if I had the necessary knowledge, I should attempt to show that all or most of these devices are common to all the arts, and to illustrate their use, particularly in music and painting. The reiteration of the 'theme' of the Venus motif, in Tannhäuser for example, corresponds to that repetition of a word, or phrase, or idea by which the poet intensifies our sense of his emotion. So the painter uses the same device for the same end—to increase the effect of his picture upon our feelings. Hazlitt shows us that in Hogarth's picture of 'The Enraged Musician' the central idea of discord is repeatedly suggested—'by the razor grinder turning his wheel; the boy with his drum, and the girl with her rattle momentarily suspended; the pursuivant blowing his horn; the shrill milkwoman; the inexorable ballad-singer with her squalling infant; the fishwomen; the chimney sweepers at the top of the chimney, and the two cats in melodious concert on the ridge of the tiles; with the bells ringing in the distance—as we see by the flags flying'; and he might have added the howling dog whose tail has been stepped upon, and the squalling parrot outside the window. He shows, too, that in 'Gin Lane' the 'theme' of the picture is reiterated again and again—'in the woman on the stairs of the bridge asleep, letting her child fall over; her ghastly companion opposite, next to death's door, with hollow famished cheeks and staring ribs; the dog fighting with the man for the bare shin-bone; the man hanging himself in a garret; the female corpse put into a coffin by the parish beadle; the men marching after a funeral, seen through a broken wall in the background; and the very houses reeling as if drunk and tumbling about the ears of the infatuated victims below, the pawnbroker's being the only one that stands firm and unimpaired'—all which helps to 'enforce the moral meant to be conveyed by each of these pieces with a richness and research of combination and artful contrast not easily paralleled in any production of the pencil or the pen'.

In Hogarth again, who as the first and almost the greatest of our English painters is the most worthy of our study, Hazlitt notes the presence of that artistic trait which I have called consistency; for example in 'Modern Midnight Conversation', the hands of the clock in the room, where some are drunk, and the rest still drinking, point to four in the morning. He even draws a parallel between the poets' use of alliteration, and Hogarth's 'continuing the red colour of the sanguine complexion and flame-coloured hair of the female Virtuoso (in the music scene in "Marriage à la Mode") into the back of the chair ' in which she is sitting. Thackeray, in the ' English Humorists ', shows how the very pictures on the walls of the room in ' Marriage à la Mode ' strike the same note with the main theme of the story.

So the skilful use of contrast marks the great master's work in all the arts. I have shown how much of its effect the finest tower of the Middle Ages owes to the contrast between the richness of its upper stage and the massive severity of its base. In every noble spire, again, the crocketed shaft and fretted pinnacles and traceried flying buttresses spring from a tower that suggests the contrasting beauty of simple strength. The principles of light and shade must be learned by the architect no less than by the painter.

Lord Tennyson records that his father, discussing with Joachim his poem ' The Revenge ', referred to the artistic effect of contrast in the quiet line,

> And the night went down and the sun smiled out far over
> the summer sea,

in the middle of the battle scene, and asked ' Could you do that on your violin ? ' Joachim's answer is not given ; but we know that he *could* have suggested by his music a sudden calm and breathing space in the midst of combat, for to the musician, not less than to the poet, contrast is a source of beauty.

However, any adequate examination of the relations between poetry and the other arts would need a better knowledge than I possess of the technique of most of the latter ; for ' all things cannot be in man, because the son of man is not immortal'. Yet I can imagine no better service to poetry than such an examination competently carried out. Since every one likes pictures and most find pleasure in music, the common indifference to poetry must be due to a failure to realize that poetry is really both. We have forgotten that poetry *is* one of the arts and, therefore, like all the rest, 'is dedicated to Joy', that there might be 'forgetfulness of evils and a truce from cares'. It should not be possible for any one who cares for art at all—and I would add to the many definitions of man that he is an art-loving animal—to be indifferent to it in any of its manifestations.

'Art for art's sake' is a mistaken principle (so far as it has any meaning at all); but one art for the sake of mere proficiency is a more mistaken and a more common one. What we should aim at is using the influence of all the arts towards development of the power to appreciate beautiful things.

I think we might try much more than we do in schools to use one art to illustrate and help in teaching another. I believe, for example, that we could often find a passage of music having the same 'theme' as a passage of poetry, and so producing the same 'mood' in the hearers. Moreover, those with musical gifts could improvise such illustrations. I remember sharing the delight of a class of boys when a visitor to the school sat down at the piano and illustrated the contrast of which I have spoken between the two stanzas of the 'Ancient Mariner' beginning:

> An orphan's curse . . .

and

> The moving moon went up the sky.

The practice of 'setting' poems as songs is a very different matter. If that can be justified at all it is not on the ground that it illustrates and emphasizes the beauty of poetry: a poem, such as 'Crossing the Bar', has its own music of the *speaking* voice, and was never conceived as *sung* sound nor meant to be translated into it; to my mind there could be no worse example of 'wasteful and ridiculous excess'; it is at least as bad as to paint the lily. I understand that Shelley's 'West Wind' has been 'set' as a song. I hope I may never hear it. But the same *theme* might doubtless be expressed, by a musician of genius, in instrumental music; Joachim could have done it on his violin.

On the other hand, it would doubtless be too much to say that verse intended to be set to music and sung should suggest the need for music when heard in the speaking voice; and yet in reading the songs of the Middle Ages we do often feel an impulse to put notes to them. Try, for example,

I sing of a maiden
That is makeless;
King of all kings
To her son she ches.

He came all so still
Where his mother was,
As dew in April
That falleth on the grass.

So most of Shakespeare's songs seem to suggest a light, airy framework—beautiful in itself, but purposely designed to be filled in, as it were, with music; they have a perfect rhythm for the purpose, simple not subtle;

they have no great weight or volume of sound, and none of the wonderful cadences of his other verse; they are indeed intended as material for the musician, and to be finished by him.

The exceptions that occur to me are 'Full Fathom Five' and 'Fear no more the heat o' the Sun', and I think that in these poetry mastered Shakespeare as it so often did, and he forgot that he was writing songs, and let his own full music escape into them. At least I love them better spoken than sung. There is too much of Shakespeare's deeper mind in them for them to be good songs.

There is a very wide, fertile and almost virgin field in the relation between poetry and painting; poetry will reveal new beauties in pictures and open the lips of those who would speak of them; and painting will help the imagination to see form and colour in words.

Comparatively few schools are within reach of picture galleries (and I fear that few of those make full use of their opportunities), but the great advance made in colour-printing has brought good reproductions of fine pictures within reach of all schools: the catalogue of the Medici Society especially should be in the hands of every teacher.

Many pictures have been specifically painted to illustrate certain poems—the rich colours and striking detail of Tennyson's early work attracted painters as they still attract children—but we are not limited in our range of illustrations by such designed parallelisms: indeed the most successful for our purpose are likely to be those in which the painter has been *separately* inspired by the same subject. For example, although Tennyson specially approved Burne Jones's 'Lady of Shalott', the deep pathos of her story is better suggested in Millais' picture of another ill-fated lady, Ophelia; so Pettie's 'Vigil' suggests the atmosphere of Sir Galahad, whose 'knees were bowed in crypt and shrine', although it was painted without reference to the poem.

It is a good exercise in art criticism to compare a picture and a poem having the same theme; to study for example, Hawker's 'Cornish Mother' and La Thargue's 'Man with the Scythe' or Keats' poem and Dicksee's picture of 'La Belle Dame Sans Merci', side by side. Children should be asked to decide which form of presentation pleases them better, which tells them most and moves them most, and to give their reasons for their views. They might also be encouraged in every school to study poetry with the school pictures in mind, and to watch for illustrative passages which might be printed on cards on the picture-frame. Below our school picture of 'Napoleon on the Bellerophon', for example, we have Shirley's 'The glories of our blood and state'; over Briton Rivière's 'Beyond Man's Footsteps' are the lines from 'Morte d'Arthur':

> Seen where the moving isles of winter shock
> By night with noises of the northern sea;
> . . . Night in a waste land, where no one comes,
> Or hath come, since the making of the world;

beneath Miss Kemp Welch's 'Colt-hunting' we have the description in 'Mazeppa' of the wild horses' dash from the forest and also Shakespeare's lines on the power of music over even 'a herd of wanton colts'; near our Arundel print of Romanino's 'The Chase' is Scott's hunting song,

'Waken lords and ladies gay'; and so with all our pictures.

Again, it is a good exercise to make a picture in words, whether in verse or prose, 'translating' a painting. But this matter belongs rather to the chapter on 'Children's Exercises'.

I know that this chapter is as sketchy and insufficient as it is short; but it is concerned with a subject on which very little has been written, and if it suggests to others some matter for further consideration its purpose will have been accomplished.

CHAPTER IX

POETRY IS FORMAL BEAUTY

A Thing of Beauty is a Joy for ever.

I SUPPOSE that most people who read so far will ask: But is there nothing in poetry but music and pictures? Granted that poetical form should be studied and appreciated, for what other good shall we seek; what of the poets' message to men; what of the meaning of the poem? And some will add: What does poetry teach?

If it were commonly accepted that poetic form *should* be studied for the sake of appreciative enjoyment, my end would have been gained and I could leave these questions to answer themselves. But that morbid growth, the examination system, which had its roots in nineteenth-century utilitarianism, has so warped our educational ideals that even poetry is expected to show 'results', some tangible effects, upon which the appraiser may lay his hand. Many teachers, I hope, would be glad to feel that their children appreciated poetry as a thing of beauty, but I fear that very few would be content to let them find in it, as Keats did, simply a joy. That, however, is the point of view I want to put in this chapter.

In good poetry there *is* something more than we have yet spoken of; it is a something that is in all good art. But it is nothing tangible, nothing that can be explained or exhibited to children. So far as words will take us we may call it an atmosphere, a glamour investing the verse, a kind of dream-light not created but proceeding; it stirs in us a sense of some mysterious meaning not expressed by the words themselves, not even consciously intended by the poet. It thrills us with the presence as of

> A shrine
> Occult, with-held, untrod.

But though we cannot explain it, it is as real a presence as life itself; those who have not felt it in poetry will have known it in the mysterious melancholy that haunts fine music, or will have seen it in the eyes of the 'Monna Lisa'. Only the Philistine cannot feel it, for ''Tis not in the World's markets bought and sold'. . .

> Hame, hame, hame, O hame fain wad I be—
> O hame, hame, hame, to my ain countree!

What is there in the repetition of a single monosyllable that has such power over the heart? No critic can tell.

> When the stars threw down their spears,
> And watered heaven with their tears . . .

and

> I will make you brooches and toys for your delight
> Of bird-song at morning and star-shine at night.
> I will make a palace fit for you and me
> Of green days in forests and blue days at sea.

That is either poetry or nonsense. We, who feel its mysterious charm, know it is poetry, though criticism, the judgement, cannot analyse it or state it in terms of music or pictures simply. But the heart knows that the lines are poetry *because it is moved by them*. This is the final test of poetry, that it communicates a mood. There is the artist's function; it has little or nothing to do with the intellect, for it presents not notions but images, that produce in us a definite state of feeling but have no meaning that can be expressed in intellectual conceptions. If the reader will only think of music instead of poetry, this paragraph will not appear so difficult. But, unfortunately, we have separated poetry from the other arts, and have almost forgotten that she, too, is Apollo's, not Minerva's, child.

The question 'What does poetry teach?' is one that could only be asked in a society which has made examinations a be-all and end-all in education. Poetry does not teach: it inspires. Those who would teach must before all things be logically clear; but the very essence of poetry is exactly what cannot be *intellectually*[1] conceived or expressed: the poet is not a schoolmaster but a prophet, and his speech is dark. I do not mean verbally obscure, like Browning; no great poet is vague any more than a great painter is indefinite; the language of Blake and Shakespeare, as has been said, is as precise as the *Book of Revelation*. But you can get no system of thought out of it. The water is clear as crystal, but it is unfathomable. Browning's language, on the other hand, is difficult, but only as Tacitus is difficult: when you have mastered his style you find that a great deal of his poetry is not poetry at all but versified philosophy. It is a deep and turbid stream, but you can get to the bottom of it and discover most of what is there.

There is a great deal of 'teaching' in Wordsworth, but the best of it is in his prose prefaces—e.g. in the preface

[1] It is true that the supreme artistic gift is never unaccompanied by great intellectual power; but the relation between them, so far from being direct and obvious as might be supposed, is profoundly obscure, an, at present, insoluble mystery.

in which he teaches that 'All good poetry is the spontaneous overflow of powerful feelings'—and all of it would have been more effective in prose than in verse.

The mistake of supposing that the teaching of a poem can be formulated is responsible for the lamentable practice of paraphrasing poetry. Paraphrasing itself as an exercise may be good intellectual discipline, like construing, but poetry cannot be translated without ceasing to exist; it is true that in a poet-translator's hands it may give birth to a new poem, as happened to Homer and Omar Khayyam, but that is neither paraphrase nor translation; it is a new creation.

The mark of all bad criticism is that it seizes on the matter rather than on the form. Dr. Johnson has been justly rebuked by Matthew Arnold for his judgement of Lycidas; but his very worst blunder was to 'suppose that no one could read Lycidas with pleasure *because the true meaning is so uncertain and remote*', and into this blunder Arnold himself fell when he charged Shelley with 'an incurable want in his poetry of sound subject matter and so of an incurable fault of unsubstantiality'. We need to get rid of this kind of criticism if poetry is again to become a national joy. Men want to be made to feel not made to think, and the only helpful criticism is that which seeks not to make them understand some supposed message or teaching but that which shows them the art and leaves them to enjoy it and get the good of it into their souls and not into their minds. Tennyson laid down the first canon of poetry when he said, speaking for all true poets, 'It doesn't matter *what* we say, if people only knew; but it matters everything *how* we say it'.

The worst thing we ever got from Germany was the Higher Criticism, not of the Bible but of Shakespeare; the misguided attempt to dissect out his theology, his philosophy, his moral teaching, his educational theory, his political thought. The Germans have made a monster of him; they have discovered that the 'Midsummer Night's Dream' is really a lay sermon—and probably by this time that the sonnets are really tracts. Dr. Johnson showed what I suppose he would now admit to be 'pure ignorance', when he blamed Shakespeare because 'he is so much more careful to please than to instruct, that he seems to write without any moral purpose'; and Emerson, with perhaps more excuse (for good criticism can hardly be expected from a nation that has produced no good poetry), gravely reproves him because he chose to give us pictures when he might have given us doctrine. But no one was mischievous enough to suggest that the man whose sweet temper could tolerate all mankind but schoolmasters was really one in disguise until Matthew Arnold brought home the idea from Germany and extended it to poetry as a whole.

Never was there a more fatal error than his 'criticism of life' theory; even when he said that Shelley's letters would last longer than his lyrics he was not more completely mistaken. What Arnold and the Germans began Browning finished—nobody read him till they did begin; and now, instead of criticism we have pure dialectical analysis, so that little boys who once cursed Vergil and all his works for his grammatical complexities now hate Keats and all his because they cannot explain his meaning to their taskmasters.

We have mistaken Martha for Mary—and she has

proved a bad stepmother to the children. The one spring of art really open to all is muddied at the source, and neither the wayfaring man nor the child will willingly drink.

The good that I seek in poetry for me and mine is the good that Keats learned from the thrush to seek in it:

> Oh, fret not after knowledge, I have none,
> And yet my song comes native with the warmth.
> Oh, fret not after knowledge, I have none,
> And yet the evening listens.

Let us try to rescue poetry at least from the examiners, that we may have one study for pure delight.

Rightly received this disposes of the other questions: art's message is a personal mystery; its meaning is infinite —a poem, a picture, a sonata, has its own meaning for every individual, and all its interpretations are but shadows of the true one. 'The meaning of any beautiful created thing is at least as much in the soul of him who looks at it as it was in his soul who wrought it.' What a poem means for each one of us, what mood it communicates to us, is a personal matter; ordinary school relations between teacher and taught will rarely permit the question.

What individual words and phrases mean is a different thing. But even here, we teachers with our everlasting questions, and our unreasoning reverence for facts, need to impose a severe restraint upon our 'explanations'; there is a vicious tendency to give explanations for their own sake and not for the sake of the children. To tell them only what they wish to know is a good rule, though its breach may often be justified—and it will make waste paper of most annotated editions for examination purposes. They always make me think of that wise child who said, 'Mother, I think I should understand if only you wouldn't explain'. Notes, as Dr. Johnson said, 'may sometimes be necessary; but they are necessary evils' at the best.

There happens to be in Lycidas an 'allusion' upon which all the annotators since Johnson have broken their teeth and which is still unexplained: What did Milton mean by his 'two handed engine at the door'? That the meaning is 'uncertain and remote' has spoiled no one's enjoyment of the poem but Johnson's. I am not sure that the very mysteriousness of the threat does not add to its effect upon us. I should like to know what he meant, but I should wish to have remained in imaginative ignorance if it was discovered that his engine was nothing very terrible after all or something that had lost its dread. Even when I was grown up I learned with regret, from an annotated school Tennyson, that 'samite' was German velvet; as a matter of fact samite is nothing of the kind; it is a stuff that is only worn in the spirit world, by White Ladies of Avenel and her 'whose robe no wrought flowers did adorn'.

Most of these 'notes' add nothing to a child's enjoyment or appreciation of poetry. I remember a long note on 'citron-shadows', from 'Recollections of the Arabian Nights', in a children's Tennyson, full of botanical information concerning *Citrus Medica*, *C. Limonum*, and *C. acida* or *C. Limetta*, but with no hint of the beauty in the word. It should be a rule without an exception that explanations are only allowable when they increase enjoyment by revealing artistic beauty. A child can enjoy

Miss Kemp Welch's picture of New Forest ponies without knowing anything of William the Conqueror or that *quercus* is Latin for an oak; and he can enjoy Matthew Arnold's beautiful vision of Apollo and the Nine in Callicles' song without knowing the names of the individual muses. Later on he may learn these things, and the knowledge may do something to make up for the inevitable loss of zest that years will bring; but it is as ridiculous as it is fatal to try to make a poem suggest for a child the ideas it suggests to the adult. Their common ground is in enjoyment of its music and pictures; the setting and the background must vary with knowledge and age.

Still more ridiculous is the attempt to force upon children details of the poet's life before they have learned to love the poet's work. Why should any one be interested to know that Shakespeare was born at Stratford, until he has become interested in the plays? Then indeed it is a holy joy to go on pilgrimage and kneel on the chancel steps before the blue ledger stone; then it is a labour of love to find out all one can about his family, to hunt for the Ardern coat in the churches of the neighbouring counties, rejoicing when you come upon its checky fess; then even the aridity of genealogical parchment will blossom for you when you discover why the new spear-charged bend of Shakespeare should be quartered with the old arrow-pierced buck's head of Saxon Bulstrode. But you must love Shakespeare first. And who that loved him could bear scraps and snippets of notes?

Let the children postpone, save up, these biographical matters to be a resource and an interest in later years;

they will not make the poetry more beautiful but the poetry will sweeten them.

As for the people who cannot find enough grammatical oakum for their children to pick, sufficiently ridiculous syntactical posers to bewilder them, in mere prose, I can only suggest that, if they cannot be prosecuted for an offence against the young, a very little stretching of the law would bring them under the blasphemy act.

The mistake of considering matter rather than form leads to further misconception in the choice of poetry for the young. Children like stories, and so it is assumed that narrative verses are the most suitable for them. Thus, on the one hand, plays of Shakespeare as *stories*, together with Mrs. Hemans' stories in verse, are selected for them to study; and on the other, 'Kubla Khan', 'L'Allegro', 'The Remote Bermudas', 'A Dream of the Unknown', 'The Highland Reaper', are neglected because they are supposed to have no childish interest. These are fundamental errors. Children like other things besides stories, and one of them is *poetry*, for its mystery and for its music and pictures, and the sensuous enjoyment they bring. Shakespeare, except in extracts and, of course, in his lyrics is *not* interesting to children: as Tennyson said of himself 'boys cannot understand Shakespeare'. His insight into the hearts of men, his knowledge of

> All pains the immortal spirit must endure,
> All weakness that impairs, all griefs that bow,

can only be appreciated by those who have known spiritual suffering and sin and have eaten the fruit of the tree of knowledge of good and evil; but they do not read 'Hamlet' to hear the story of a murder and its punishment, but to weigh with him the known ills of this life against the unknown ones of a possible life to come; nor 'The Tempest' for a tale of intrigue and usurpation, but to learn how Hamlet might have emerged scorched but serene from the fires if he had been Prospero or William Shakespeare.

Narrative verse is very seldom good poetry; Scott's Lays, as everybody knows, are far inferior to his prose narratives and, as poetry, 'Proud Maisie' is worth them all except 'Flodden Field'. The best parts of them, as of Macaulay's poems, are not narrative at all but lists of magic names:

> Pibroch of Donuil Dhu,
> Pibroch of Donuil,
> Wake thy wild voice anew,
> Summon Clan-Connel.

Or pictures, that for all their truth to Scottish scenery, are seen by him and by us through Keats's magic casement.

Even the ballad, which some one has said, perhaps hastily, to be the lowest form of poetry, does not really tell a story; it does a better thing for us: it sets us wondering and imagining many possible stories. What is the real story of Helen of Kirkconnel? Or of the knight in the 'Twa Corbies'? or of La Belle Dame Sans Merci? or of Sir Hugh in William Morris's 'Shameful Death'? or of Browning's 'Patriot'? We are given a scene or two and left not with a story but with a riddle. That is Shakespeare's method, though it is not always Chaucer's.

It is no more a *poet's* function than it is a painter's to tell a tale; each gives us pictures and leaves us to interpret them or weave stories about them for ourselves, or simply to enjoy them with a purely sensuous pleasure. The pictures in the 'Blessed Damosel', for example, delight the sense by their beauty, although neither the logical connexion between them, which we call the 'meaning', is appreciated by the mind, nor their mystic symbolism even suspected. We must choose poetry not for the sake of stories, but that our young men may see visions and our children may dream dreams.

Let children read narrative verse by all means and let them write it, but do not let them suppose, as they are sometimes led to suppose, that they are enjoying poetry when they are simply amusing themselves with a tale. For my sins it has more than once happened to me to hear a series of selections from the 'Ancient Mariner' read to children, followed by a demand that they should 'write the substance of the story in their own words and say what it teaches us'. To such base uses may we come when exegesis is mistaken for criticism and the marble is thought to be the statue.

Another consideration that misleads teachers to choose poetry for its subject and substance is the moral one. Wilde's unfortunate remark that 'all art is immoral' must not blind us to the fact that most of what he said on art is true; those who are ever seeking in poetry for direct moral instruction would do well to read his 'Intentions', for it is certain that they are farther from the truth than he, even in his most mocking moments.

Art has really no more to do with morality than with the intellect. It speaks to something in us that is older than either, that existed in Eden before the Fall.

Morality is not feeling, like poetry, but willing. Art may move the feelings as sex does, but is no more an evil; the evil is in the will, not in the emotions. Where there is no knowledge there may be innocence, but there is no morality. Ruskin rightly complained of his own upbringing that it was designed to make him 'by protection innocent instead of by practice virtuous': he might have said 'ignorance' and 'will' for 'protection' and 'practice'. Morality, like patriotism, is a poor thing when blind.

There are many things, both in art and nature, to be admired for their beauty yet not to be desired for their wholesomeness. I do not of course mean that we should read 'Venus and Adonis' or the *Decameron* to school children any more than we should give briony berries to babies, simply because they are beautiful. But I do mean very decidedly that we should choose our children's poems for their beauty of form first and only negatively on account of their matter; and also that we should strive to make them understand that 'art is a way of saying a thing', and that art criticism is concerned not with the matter but with the manner of expression.

Judged by its substance, a great deal of the most beautiful poetry is worse than worthless—

> Vivamus, mea Lesbia, atque amemus
> Rumoresque senum severiorum
> Omnes unius aestimemus assis.
> Soles occidere et redire possunt:
> Nobis cum semel occidit brevis lux,
> Nox est perpetua una dormienda.
> Da mi basia mille . . .

The *doctrine* is as pernicious as the music of its

expression is tenderly beautiful. What can be more mischievous teaching than the whole burden of Fitz-Gerald's 'Rubaiyat'—

> Ah, fill the cup, what boots it to repeat
> How time is slipping underneath our feet;
> Unborn to-morrow and dead yesterday—
> Why fret about them if to-day be sweet?

Yet where can its delicious melancholy be matched—unless it be by Swinburne—

> From too much love of living,
> From hope and fear set free,
> We thank with brief thanksgiving
> Whatever Gods may be
> That no life lives for ever;
> That dead men rise up never;
> That even the weariest river
> Winds, somewhere, safe to sea.

Are we to lose such music as that, because it enshrines a false doctrine? Art has nothing to do with absolute truth; it shows truth coloured by the artist's mood, seen through the medium of the artist's mind. It is no more in the purpose or the power of art to 'show us things as they really are' than it is within the power of science. We can never know things as they really are. But we can know things as the world knows them for the practical purposes of our material life, and we can know things as the artist sees them for the enjoyment of our imaginative life without confusing the two aspects. To seek for doctrine in poetry *is* to confuse the two.

It is not the poet's part to teach us but to make us feel, to share with him his intuitive experience of the varied heart of man, and so to widen and deepen our humanity by imaginative sympathy.

Queen Victoria, who represented her age almost as well as Elizabeth did hers, admired the symbolized morality of Tennyson's 'Idylls'; but her views on art were about as edifying as her predecessor's on morality—she also admired and encouraged the activities of Sir Edgar Boehm. But Tennyson really knew better; it is significant that he was always reticent and even irritated when questioned about the symbolism of his 'Idylls': he knew, and said in a poem that will be loved when the 'Idylls' are long forgotten, what Shakespeare and Keats knew, and Gray did not, that the beauty of the summer flower, the beauty of the poet's dream, is an end in itself, not a means of teaching morality.

I believe that Madame de Staël's saying that 'Morality is in the nature of things' is profoundly true, but I know that morality is not in the nature of poetry. For the world of art is not the world of things but of the imagination. In the world of things, as butchers, bakers, and candlestick-makers, we have to live our material lives; as citizens we must submit to be bound by conventions; even as parents we must remember that, the world being what it is, our sons will be

> Neither children nor gods,
> But men in a world of men.

There is fine romance in tallow; but you cannot keep a customer waiting for his candles while you dream of bucking steers on the pampas with John Masefield; the butcher in *Chuzzlewit*, who cut the steak slowly because

> The meat was a picture for painters to study,
> The fat was so white and the lean was so ruddy,

and he delighted to admire it: who insisted on putting it carefully into Ruth's pocket himself—'for meat', he said with some emotion, 'should be humoured and not drove', probably went bankrupt, and certainly never became Sir Joseph Loins.[1]

Yet 'the daily round, the common task' will *not* furnish all we need to ask; and the only god it will bring us nearer to is the god of Mammon:

> Shop each day, and all day long?
> Friend, your good angel slept, your star
> Suffered eclipse, Fate did you wrong;
> From where these kinds of treasures are
> There should our hearts be—Christ, how far!

As a material being, 'since flesh must live', I must *act* for a part of my existence as a producer or purveyor of material things: but also, above and beyond all that, 'I am a man, and I desire to experience all that men can feel, to know all human moods'; so that I may say with Ulysses—

> I will drink
> Life to the lees: all times I have enjoy'd
> Greatly, have suffered greatly, both with those
> That lov'd me, and alone; on shore and when
> Thro' scudding drifts the rainy Hyades
> Vext the dim sea:—I am become a name
> For always roaming with a hungry heart—
> . . . . Life piled on life
> Were all too little, and of one to me
> Little remains: but every hour is saved
> From that eternal silence, something more
> A bringer of new things.

[1] With a coat of three loins proper, on a field argent gouttée de sang, to blazon on his meat carts.

Therefore I will love the still, sad music of Omar,

The player upon plaintive strings,

no less than the cheerful brass of Ben Ezra, and will wish that my soul should flee before the Hound of Heaven with Francis Thompson's as well as be lifted to the golden doors upon St. Agnes' Eve; and I will yield my spirit to the mood of the Indian Serenade, and try also to bring it into communion with Sir Galahad; and the passion of Cleopatra shall be as real and wonderful to me as the devotion of Cordelia.

The practical man, who is often a tailor, and always a fractional part of a whole man, will scoff at the unreality of imaginative experience: there is no other reality; actual events are real only to the imagination. Denis and Gerard wandered through Europe together and shared the same experience: it left the one as it found him—a mere soldier;[1] it made of the other a man fit to be the father of Erasmus, because it found him a poet, one 'of imagination, all compact', and he made poetry of all he saw. Those who actually stood round the body of Marguerite's father and saw her little letter taken from his dead hand did not feel the pathos of the scene that Austin Dobson makes us see in 'Before Sedan'; the men who brought home the wagon through the darkening lanes on a winter nightfall, and saw the tall man in the flesh, felt little of the gloom without, and nothing of the deeper gloom within; *they* only saw the 'real' things; but *we* see a great poet's vision of them.

The practical man, again, remembering that visions in the Bible were usually a guide to conduct, may ask

[1] Denis's one *experience* was his love for Gerard.

what the poet would have us *do*: he might as well ask the flowers and the birds the same question: he might as well expect Turner's 'Rain, Steam, and Speed' to help him like a diagram in a problem of practical engineering. We have lost the truth so long that this will seem a hard saying, and most parsons would denounce it as 'contrary to the teaching of religion and of Aristotle'; is not conduct three-fourths of life? and is not poetry a guide to conduct? The answer to both questions should be an emphatic denial. Conduct may be three-fourths of life, or more, to an ant or a rising greengrocer; but it is a far smaller part of the life of a man:

> What is a man,
> If his chief good and market of his time
> Be but to sleep and feed? a beast, no more.
> Sure he that made us with such large discourse,
> Looking before and after, gave us not
> That capability and god-like reason
> To fust in us unus'd.

Contemplation as well as conduct, the life of the imagination as well as the life of action, is a large and essential part of the life of man, and it is with this part that the arts are solely concerned.

Never did the middle-class Victorian mind find more characteristic utterance than in Matthew Arnold's assertion that conduct was the largest part of life, and that great poetry depended upon great actions. We must go back, and if we cannot yet receive the saying that

> To me the meanest flower that blows can give
> Thoughts that do often lie too deep for tears.

let us appeal from Matthew sober to Matthew intoxicated with the spirit of poetry: let us see how small a part conduct played in the life of his scholar gipsy and how little the beauty of his poem depends upon action.

The scholar gipsy, like Stevenson's vagabond, who asked but the heaven above him and the open road before, and like Mr. Polly, who burnt down his house, and threw all social responsibilities to the winds, that he might live 'according to nature', forgot that man has a dual nature: they forgot that he has a duty to his own body and to other bodies, just as the millionaire forgets that he has a soul. But whereas the millionaire, like Browning's Venetians, does often succeed in delivering himself from his soul,[1] this too, too solid flesh is with us to the end, and its demands must condition our conduct; it is futile and hopeless, and immoral, to seek to evade them. We may hope—it is the highest teaching of Ruskin and Carlyle, the most inspired, if not the greatest men of modern times—that men may come more and more to understand that it is

> Poor vaunt of life indeed
> Were men but formed to feed
> On joy, to solely seek, and find, and feast,
> Such feasting ended, then
> As sure an end to men—
> Irks care the cropful bird? Frets doubt the maw-crammed beast?

and that they may realize how relatively small a part material things need play in the full life of man.

Meanwhile those critics are utterly mistaken who would

[1] 'What of soul was left I wonder when the kissing had to stop?'

have us find in poetry a guide to conduct in this world instead of an ideal existence in a world of the mind, who would persuade us that art shows us things as they are, when it really reveals to us a refuge from things as they are.[1] 'This world', said Novalis, 'is not a dream; but it ought to become one.' We must realize, and make our children realize, that poetry, *as poetry*, is not a guide to conduct but a solace to life. I said *as poetry* because the words of the poets do very often express the conclusions of the moralist; but equally often they can no more be reconciled with the conventions of life than could Don Quixote's romanticism. The kingdom of poetry is not of this world. Its allegiance is 'a devotion to something afar From the sphere of our sorrow'.

Men have always felt this and some, like Plato, have therefore desired to suppress poetry or at least to exclude it from education. But Plato, too, falls into the common error of supposing that poetry, as poetry, is doctrine, and that poetry, as poetry, is to be judged by the reason. Yet once he actually has the truth on his tongue and cannot hear it: 'what a poor appearance the ideas of the poets make when stripped of the colours which music puts upon them and recited in simple prose'. What he fails to see is that judgement of ideas and enjoyment of the manner of their presentation are totally different functions.

Poetry, like rhetoric, is beautiful form; and judgement of the matter presented is an entirely different thing from appreciation of the art which presents it.

Poetry expresses opinions that we ought to accept and act upon, and opinions that we ought to reject; but this

[1] In their material aspect.

discrimination has nothing to do with art criticism or artistic enjoyment. Because this truth is not realized, nine-tenths of us are in danger of rejecting poetry altogether as roundabout prose, and the rest of seeking philosophy where we should be finding pure enjoyment and intellectual *rest.* Ruskin saw better than Plato the true attitude towards art. He shows us three points of view: the first, Peter Bell's, of 'the man who perceives rightly because he does not feel, and to whom the primrose is very accurately the primrose because he does not love it'; the second, of the man that Plato seems to think typical 'who perceives wrongly because he feels, and to whom the primrose is anything else than a primrose—a star, or a sun, or a fairy's shield or a forsaken maiden'; and then lastly, 'there is the man who perceives rightly in spite of his feelings and for whom the primrose is for ever nothing else than itself—a little flower apprehended in the very plain and leafy fact of it, whatever and how many soever the associations and passions may be that crowd around it'.

That is the point of view we should desire for our children.

If we would only bring to poetry simply 'a heart that watches and receives', would leave the intellect and all its problems outside the door as we do at a picture gallery or a music room, we might begin to understand something of what art meant in happier ages. Or if we cannot do that for ourselves let us try to save it from being 'sicklied o'er with the pale cast of thought' at least in our children's sight, so that they may find in it the gates of Eden still open, a world of pure feeling and a refuge from the world of action and of thought.

In poetry as in religion, we have been over-anxious for our souls, we can do nothing without thinking how it shall profit them, we are too ready to believe that a man by taking thought can add to his spiritual stature.

It is profoundly true that the great poet is also the great seer, and that his poetry will 'do us good'; but that is not the message men need to-day; the few are already too conscious of it, and the many have heard it too often to believe it.

The first lesson for us to learn in the schools is Dryden's, that 'poetry only instructs as it delights'; the truth the world has forgotten is not that poetry is edifying but that it is delightful. If we can help children to enjoy the art of it, its music and its pictures, so that they will read it for this alone, we may leave the poets to speak to them without any schoolmaster-interpreter, remembering that those who seek beauty only will find truth also.

CHAPTER X

CHILDREN'S EXERCISES

'What shall it profit a man, if he gain the whole world and lose his own soul?'

'I want to know a butcher paints,
A baker rimes for his pursuit,
Candlestick-maker much acquaints
His soul with song, or haply mute
Blows out his brains upon the flute.'

THE one great purpose of the poetry lesson is to help the children to appreciate poetry so that they may learn to love it and to wish to read it for themselves in after years. But a secondary, though very important, purpose is to develop their own creative power: we must help them not merely to enjoy poetry but to write clearly and attractively themselves, with the poets as their models.

Many teachers will reply that it is hard enough to teach children to write grammatically without expecting them to write poetically. That is the traditional point of view and with it I wish to deal, for I believe it to be radically wrong. To write brightly and picturesquely is far better than to write merely grammatically, and though it is far more difficult for adults, is really natural and easy to children. For the child is a poet by nature. Only yesterday, in marking some exercises in original verse, I found in a stanza written by a boy of twelve, a barber's son, an average boy in all respects, the line:

Rooks at work in pairs . . .
And merry are the sandy hares.

Now that is pure poetry. There is a blemish in sound in

the lack of vowel-variety, especially in the recurrence of the terminal *y*, but the epithets are perfect. 'Merry' has life and movement; 'sandy' has colour: and each is *le mot juste*; they hit the very essence of the hare, body and spirit, its inward being and its outward seeming. Moreover, and this is a subtle but vital matter, they are emotional words; they express the effect and impression the hare makes on the spirit, or the feelings, not what he is to the mind or understanding. Older people may perhaps have a little difficulty in appreciating the distinction, for it is very hard to explain; but those who look at the hare to *understand* him rather than to *enjoy* him would think of neither of those words—certainly not merry—but of more 'scientific' ones.

This is not a single instance but a typical childish expression. I hope to induce some of my readers to experiment for themselves, and they will find that when children are given scope for the exercise of the poetic power, which is the special gift of their time of life, the results are surprising. I am not speaking only, or even mainly, of original verse, but of the use of imagery, of the figures of speech and of pictorial epithets in descriptive essays, and of imaginative writing generally.

In the average school neither the subjects commonly set for essays nor the methods of treating them are such as will call into play the peculiar powers of children; they are too 'grown up', too conventional, very often wretchedly hackneyed—one of the most deplorable things in the elementary schools is the existence of what may almost be called an elementary school 'style'. This is in part a legacy from those dreadful days when the child was supplied with a card on which was printed a 'model' essay on Thrift or Punctuality or Coke upon the basis of which he had to construct an 'original' essay for himself; only in the leading articles of contemporary provincial newspapers could the style of these models be matched. But it is more largely due to the still prevalent practice of 'composition from the blackboard'. The teacher chooses a subject, discusses it at length with the class, plans out—with their co-operation he fondly believes—a scheme or skeleton of the essay, and then invites sentences from individual children, selections from which, according to his taste, he writes on the blackboard, duly correcting the grammar. Finally, the children copy the concoction into their exercise books. The hardest lesson for a teacher to learn is that children's intuition is often wiser than his own learning: he may write a grammatically correct essay, but the children's, if they are given a free hand, will be much more interesting and attractive, because their ideas and their style are fresh and unconventional, however inaccurate. We are too apt to put our own ideas into their heads, and then demand them at their hands. Not our style but the poets' should be our children's model.

Abstract subjects, like 'Honesty' or 'A stitch in time saves nine' and subjects in their commercial aspects, e. g. 'Salt' or 'Railways', though very popular with teachers are not suitable for children; they involve word-spinning without interest, whereas we need above all things to awaken the zest for self-expression, and the sense of delight that comes with power over words. Moreover the child thinks in images, not in concepts, and so can write most naturally on concrete subjects. Above all, abstract subjects give a child no opportunity of measuring the value of his work, of testing its practical success: his teacher may mark his essay Good or Poor, but he himself has no means of criticizing the judgement.

Picture-making, the writing of descriptions, and the use of figures of speech, put his work to the test of practical success; if he writes a picture of a given place or thing, or finds a simile to describe a colour or a shape, or a metaphor to express an essential characteristic, he knows, independently of his teacher's approval, whether his work is accurate or not. Moreover, he can submit such work to the judgement of his peers and contemporaries—his fellow pupils.

I have found it good training in prose-description to ask boys to write a picture of some person, place, or building known to all of us—for example a school-fellow, or a chapel, or a street-corner—and afterwards to read their description aloud, and judge its success by the number of their class-mates who recognized the portrait. Such an exercise helps them to realize the importance of seizing essentials and of choosing the most striking epithets to describe them. To show them how great writers have attempted the same sort of task, I have read such pictures as Defoe's of Crusoe and of his house, Boswell's of Johnson (Globe Ed., e. g. pp. 166, 690), Fuller's of Henry V or Elizabeth, Clarendon's of a bull-fight, Miss Mitford's of a cottage in 'Our Village', Dickens's of Mr. Wemmick's house or Miss Havisham's room, Kingsley's of a tropical river, Scott's of Meg Merrilies or Cedric's Hall—to take but a few random examples. Any one who will note suitable passages in his own reading will soon have a plentiful list.

Until boys have learned to write clear and life-like

pictures of persons and things known to them, they cannot be expected to produce good essays in history or geography; if they cannot describe clearly their brothers and the places they have seen, how shall they make clear to others the figure of William the Conqueror, or a lumber-camp, or a mediaeval street? But when they can describe things seen, they may go on to paint things imagined. As an exercise leading up to this I have exposed a picture to observation for one minute, then removed it, and required the class to write a description which they subsequently compared with the original picture. For this purpose, posters, in these days of really artistic posters, will be found very useful, and may readily be obtained.

These descriptive exercises immediately call into play the children's power to use the figures of speech. We have seen that the simile, particularly, is often used by poets to supply deficiencies of language; how much more valuable must it be, as an aid to expressing themselves, to children whose vocabulary is naturally limited? They like, as much as, or even more than older people, to do something, even if it is only writing, *well*, but they have not the necessary stock of epithets. But the simile is such a simple figure, and yet so strong in pictorial effect, that they can easily use it to supply their lack of descriptive words.

Even the youngest children may be asked, in describing, say, the strength of a man, to think of a thing possessing strength in the highest degree, and so to write 'This man was as strong as a bull' or 'had the strength of a horse', instead of simply 'was very strong'; or in describing a girl's eyes, they may be asked to think where their colour may be found, and instead of saying vaguely they were blue or brown, to write 'blue like the chicory', or 'as the cornflowers', or 'brown as a peat-stream', or 'grey like the sea'. One will perhaps say 'brown as my father's pipe' and thus give an opportunity for discussion on incongruous ideas.

Children enjoy exercising their poetical powers in the invention of metaphors. I have asked the little ones, for example, to 'find a new name for the baby which will tell how precious she is' (i.e. to give her the name of a symbol of preciousness); and they have written, 'Our baby is a pearl', or 'a jewel' or 'a treasure'. Or I have asked them to find 'new names' for flowers, and trees, and animals, for example a name for the oak which will tell he is the chief of the trees, or for the lion which will proclaim him above all the beasts, or for the elm which will describe its hugeness.

The most elementary exercise with metaphors is to take a simile and compress it into a metaphor. For example, if children cannot readily find a 'new name' for a lily, they will perhaps suggest she is 'like a queen' and so discover that we can call her 'a queen of flowers'.

And this brings me to the figure which all children use by a deep-rooted instinct—personification.

It is not an unusual exercise in some schools to allow children to write life-stories of inanimate things in the first person. This practice might be greatly extended and applied to essays on subjects where the third person is commonly used; a child will write a better account of the Saxon land system if he writes as a serf or a thegn, or of monasticism if he writes as a monk, or of Flodden

Field if he writes as an archer, than he could do speaking in the third person as a detached observer: he *feels* his subject more, i.e. he writes as a poet. Of course he must learn to use the ordinary form in time, but when he has gained the sense of controlling language he will have no difficulty over a little matter like that. Moreover this form of writing will be a far better test of the knowledge he has assimilated: he cannot, as children so often do, reproduce chunks of undigested text-book strung on a thin string of his own composition. He will thus learn the first great lesson for all who write—that one must first have a clear perception of something to say and a strong desire to say it.

I believe that the older children, especially, in our schools write a great deal of vague, woolly, colourless, cheerless stuff to order on subjects in which they do not feel the least interest. But writing, to the young, should never be a task but a pleasure, the gratification of desire, and it can only be such when the writer is interested in his subject. In order to stimulate this zest I encourage my own boys, in their last six months at school, to leave the ordinary school-books and school syllabuses and to browse in the public library and choose subjects of study for themselves, to obtain from the library the books that interest them and bring them to school for the purpose. To this privilege I attach only one condition: that they convince me by their essays that they are really interested in *something*; I do not care much what it is. I have boys who read Boutell's *Heraldry* in the history lessons and go out of school to sketch coats of arms in the drawing lessons, and others who study Kelly's *Guide to Oxfordshire* when the time-table says 'geography' and are brass-rubbing in a village church when it says 'handwork'.

What a boy *knows* when he leaves school at fourteen must necessarily be very little and, fortunately, matters very little. But what a boy *thinks* about the value of knowledge and the purposes of study, whether or not he has formed some intellectual interests, if he has begun to distinguish between the style of R. L. Stevenson and that of Mr. Le Queux—these things will matter to him till his dying day and will matter to his children after him.

Pictures of the images of things personified are good exercises alike for the imaginative life—which is *human* life—and for developing literary power. Children who have appreciated Keats's 'Ode to Autumn' or Longfellow's 'Building of the Ship' will like to attempt for themselves a picture of Winter or the Thames 'as he looked when I saw him', and they will do it with a freshness of detail, an instinct for pictorial effect, and a vivid use of simile and of colour surprising to older people. I am constantly getting essays of this kind from children which I could never have written myself. But we are too apt to measure children's powers by our own, and that is why we fail to make the best use of them; we set them the kind of work that we ourselves think we can do well.

The repression of instinct which comes with age makes apostrophe, except perhaps of golf balls, an unusual exercise with adults. To children it is a natural and interesting one—Jean Ingelow's child in 'Seven' might be any child. They can write an 'Address to the Sun' and afterwards compare it with Tennyson's 'Hymn of

Akbar', or to the moon and compare it with Shelley, or to the Thames and then read Denham's lines, or to a lamb and read Blake, or to a skylark and read Hogg. I do not think children are allowed, anything like so frequently as they should be, to bring their own work to the touch of good writers, or even to realize that great writers have thought 'worth while' such themes as they themselves are interested to write upon.

I believe that formal grammar teaching in an uninflected language like ours is more useless than oakum picking, and that correct syntax will come by the incidental correction of errors; but this use of apostrophe, by employing the second person singular, will incidentally give opportunities, not often found, to ensure the proper agreement between pronoun and verb.

Children may try not merely to emulate the poets but even to compete with them. That is not so ridiculous as it may sound, for to have failed is to have a criterion of success. But actually, if a good deal of poetry is a rhetorical presentation of a point of view, children may find good training in attempting to set forth the opposite point of view. I will give as an illustration an exercise I lately set to some senior boys. I gave them the following passage of Hazlitt on Coleridge's sermon:

'The sermon was upon peace and war; upon Church and State—not their alliance but their separation—on the spirit of the world and the spirit of Christianity, not as the same but as opposed to one another. He talked of those who had "inscribed the Cross of Christ on banners dripping with human gore". He made a poetical and pastoral excursion, and to shew the fatal effects of war, drew a striking contrast between the simple shepherd boy, driving his team afield, or sitting under the hawthorn piping to his flock "as though he should never be old", and the same poor country lad, crimped, kidnapped, brought into town, made drunk at an alehouse, turned into a wretched drummer-boy, with his hair sticking on end with powder and pomatum, a long cue at his back, and tricked out in the loathsome finery of the profession of blood.'

Every one, at least every one competent to form an opinion, will admire that passage as art, as a noble and moving expression of a mood and an effective exposition of a point of view. (It is prose, but Southey's 'Blenheim' or Austin Dobson's 'Before Sedan' would have been equally suitable for my purpose.) Art-criticism will be at one in admiring its *form*. But as to its *matter* opinions and prejudices will be strongly opposed. Some will say that all children should read, mark, learn, and inwardly digest it: others will hold that no English child should see it. I asked my boys to examine it and, using it as a model, to attempt to set forth the opposite argument, the justification of war, its nobler aspects, the effect of discipline on the idle and debauched. For I believe that those who best appreciate rhetoric as an art will be least likely to surrender their judgement to it.

I would emphasize the observation that many of the exercises suggested in this chapter have an educational value that extends far beyond 'English' even in its widest meaning; they involve training in exact observation such as we usually associate with the science, nature-study and drawing lessons; they mean (what education ought always to mean) making environment a constant mental and imaginative stimulus.

And so I return to the original problem of this chapter,

how can we preserve the poetic clearness of vision and directness of description that are the child's birthright, while widening his range of experience, of thought, and vocabulary; how can we save him from developing, as most of us do, conventional views of things and a hackneyed style? Is it a law of nature, or only an unhappy and preventible accident that, while the youth

> By the vision splendid
> Is on his way attended,
> At length the man beholds it die away
> And fade into the light of common day?

I shall make no apology for quoting again, as the first principle of education, that 'it is the first distemper of learning when men study words and not things', for I am convinced that a great deal of our teaching in history, geography, mathematics, even science, is conventional, mechanical, and so unfruitful because that wisest word of one of the wisest of Englishmen remains still unregarded in our schools. Unreality is the root of all evil in teaching. Little children who have never seen the sea learn glib definitions of bights and promontories like parrots; older children who could not distinguish at sight a forty acre field from a ten pole allotment, work long calculations in square miles, and tell you that 'area is length multiplied by breadth', never realizing either that if you multiply 'length' you get more length, or that you cannot multiply by yards or miles of breadth; nearly all children learn the results of the Norman Conquest, and never, knowingly, see a Norman church or castle. As for the ridiculous humbug miscalled 'science' in some of our (still more miscalled) 'higher grade' schools, Mr. Wells has dealt with it, but with too light a hand. The one vital purpose of science, in general education, is to develop a scientific outlook on things, a habit of mind that makes men observant of natural phenomena and curious about their meaning. School science, like school arithmetic, is often mere conjuring and juggling with matters the children never hear of except in the schoolroom; they infer that 'science' is concerned with sundry evil-smelling, mysterious things in bottles, and would hear with astonishment that the boy scout who learns, say, first to distinguish all the finches by the bar on their wings and next to deduce from it their descent from a common ancestor; or who makes a collection of the labiate flowers and then, by watching the bees at work in them, discovers the purpose of the lip and the hood, and, by observing the sunlight on their leaves, the reason for the plants' pyramidal form; who can tell by the kind of mud on his brother's boots the way he went on his Sunday walk—is making a real approach to science: and making it, too, by the natural road followed by the primitive fathers of science.

> Come forth into the light of *things*,
> Let Nature be your teacher.

It is certain that poetry at least can never be properly appreciated unless it is realized as the mirror of nature. A child can appreciate

> His hair was crisp, and black, and long,
> His face was like the tan,

or even

> The sunset that doth glorify
> The orange and pale-violet evening sky,

although he knows little of nature outside the streets—

but even so not unless habits of observation have been encouraged; but the full beauty of 'Birds in the high Hall garden' is only revealed to one who has heard the rooks say 'Maud, Maud, Maud, Maud', and the thrushes answer 'He-re, he-re, he-re', and *seen* the sleeping daisies rosy. Unless poetry, like so much else in schools, is to be 'words! words! words!' it must be an out-of-door study, and must go hand in hand with observation of nature. The first service of the poets for us is to find us words to voice our feelings; what children feel most is the wonder of the constant stream of impressions from the outside world; and, like Adam in the garden, their first need is for language to express the effect of things upon them. God showed the creatures he had made to Adam that he might name and describe them. Science and art are twins in the cradle of the primitive mind however far apart they afterwards grow. To observe the external world and to express the feelings aroused by it are the first functions of the mind of man. The study of nature, and of poetry, under the guidance of those who know and love both, are necessities of life to all children, and must be carried on side by side. Contact with the one will keep alive the divine gift of wonder, and contact with the other will preserve freshness of style.

And here arises the question of learning by heart. Why should children learn by heart, what should they learn, and how? Most of us are too ready, and too sure, in answering.

I need not discuss the old idea that learning by heart trains the memory, since it has been exploded with the rest of the 'special faculties' doctrine; the only faculty improved by learning poetry is the faculty for learning more poetry. But I fancy that with that theory has gone the only ground on which many teachers could justify their practice. How many teachers still retain the stores of verse they themselves once learned to order? How many have forgotten them without regret? How few hold them as a dear possession and recall them as a sweet memory? How few add to them from day to day?

Those who have forgotten most of the poetry they ever learnt themselves still insist in forcing on children a fixed number of lines to be learned yearly—and forgotten the year after. Stores unused are useless, and soon vanish, as if they had never been. Experience has convinced me that the value of the poetry children learn is in inverse ratio to the trouble taken in acquiring it; and that the vast majority of what is learnt lies absolutely sterile in the memory till it gradually fades out of it. Lines learnt as Tom Sawyer learned them, for recitation at the school concert or the inspector's visit, will be forgotten when the occasion has passed.

Those parts of what we learn are most fruitful that are constantly brought back to the stream of consciousness by our favourite subject of thought, or by the stimulus of our surroundings. To a man often pondering over the spiritual state of present-day England the whole of Wordsworth's greatest sonnet will return again and again; but a child who has learnt it all will recall spontaneously only

> The sea that bares her bosom to the moon,
> The winds that will be howling at all hours,
> And are upgathered now like sleeping flowers,

because as yet he lives in a world of images, not of reflection. Yet I think we might be glad indeed to feel that the sight of the sea, or the sound of the wind, would bring those magnificent lines into the mind of a child we cared for.

Here, I believe, is an approachable ideal. Let us train the children to look, in every poem they study, for some beautiful passage to remember and quote in the presence of the things that inspired it; let us encourage them to make a habit of noting these in their commonplace books —which is half-way to knowing them by heart—so that gradually

> Meadow, grove, and stream,
> The earth and every common sight

shall have its own association with a poet's phrase; so that when the vision splendid fades, if fade it must, the youth who daily farther from the east must fare shall take some of the glory with him on his way.

But I prefer to believe, with Ruskin, that the vision need not fade; it did not fade for the Greeks, and those who love the Greek muses seem to preserve it still—I am not thinking only of Keats, but of 'Greats' men I have known, who seem to have learned from them the secret of

> Glad perennial youth,

and who will die young because they will never grow old. But they, alone, in English education to-day, understand that studies serve *first* for delight. Certainly there is no other reason for learning poetry.

A good deal may be done to reduce the drudgery of learning by heart—for to ordinary memories it is a drudgery—by better considered methods than now obtain. The once universal practice of simultaneous repetition is discouraged by the school inspectors, and is therefore dying out; the inspectorial objection to it is that it cultivates, not individual expression, but a common sing-song tone. From my experience of exaggerated, over-inflected individual expression I am inclined to prefer the common chant as the lesser of two evils. But the real ground of objection to the simultaneous method is that it allows the mind of the individual to wander instead of concentrating its power; a class will repeat thirty or forty lines in chorus once or twice a week throughout a whole term, and half the members will not know the passage at the end of it.

I have found the old misused and now despised exercise of dictation a very valuable means towards getting poetry by heart; there is no such thing as 'memory training', but forming habits of thought is the very basis of education, and dictation is the best of all exercises for forming the habit of listening with concentrated attention. Unfortunately, it is generally used as a mere spelling exercise; three or four words are repeated three or four times, syllable by syllable, with an altogether inhuman attempt at clearness of enunciation, and the children are then required to write them down in correct spelling. (I know nothing, in a world of wonders, more remarkable than an old-time teacher 'giving out dictation'.)

But the newer school, while rightly condemning such a method as mechanical and unintelligent, is equally wrong in abandoning dictation altogether; rightly used it can train children so to concentrate their minds that they can retain long phrases in the memory after hearing them once or twice or seeing them for a few moments.

I have found that average children, when once they have learned to listen with full concentration, have no difficulty in writing down a couplet after hearing it once, or a rimed quatrain recited twice or thrice according to length and difficulty of subject. So if a stanza of ordinary length is exposed on a blackboard for 60–90 seconds, children who have learned to use that time with concentrated energy can reproduce the lines accurately from memory. This does not mean that they will thereafter retain them permanently; but they will have very little trouble in doing so; a week afterwards they will be able to rewrite the quatrain after a single hearing, or to write two stanzas instead of one.

Rime arrangement should always be used as a help in getting a stanza by heart; the rimes may be made a kind of prompter suggesting the lines to come. Any one who has once made himself thoroughly familiar with the architectural form of the sonnet, or of a long stanza like Spenser's, or Keats's, or Arnold's, will learn a whole stanza or sonnet more readily and more surely than half a dozen lines of irregular or unrimed verse. Those who have not realized this should experiment with a stanza of the Scholar Gipsy, a peculiarly suitable stanza for the purpose, because its rime arrangement is so subtle that it is possible to learn the sestet like blank verse, without noticing the rime at all; but when once the rimes are used as a clue the time taken to learn a stanza will be halved at least.

The greatest difficulty in learning by heart, especially for children, is to retain the 'logical sequence' of the parts except in verses which tell a story. Now no great poetry depends on the mere thread of a narrative, and so long passages are hard to learn. I know every separate stanza of the 'Elegy' or of 'The Blessed Damosel', for instance, and yet I am sure I could not recite them in the right order, and so I should fail to satisfy the school inspector that I 'knew' them. For, unfortunately, there is a type of inspector who can judge only by word-perfect recitation whether or not work has been done. Any dunce can drive verses into children's heads for another dunce to get them out again, and dunces have been doing both since first there were schools; but they cannot make them stay there when their victim has escaped their ferule; and in driving the poetry into the head they usually drive the love of it out of the heart.

Let me be quite frank about this: poetry is taught in all schools, men are born with a *natural* appetite for it; and not one in a thousand learns, nor one in a hundred even reads, a line when his school-days are over.

There is something wrong somewhere. Examiners and inspectors, and teachers who live only to propitiate them, have turned what should be a natural joy into an artificial drudgery, by cramming the hapless children with 'meanings and allusions' and with 'passages for recitation'.

I should be the last to undervalue learning by heart; I know that the more poetry a boy learns, the better and the happier for him, and that no poem can be fully appreciated until it is known by heart. But unless we can induce him to learn for pure delight, our efforts will be a curse to him and not a blessing. Only the labour we delight in can physic its own pain; a child who has learnt poetry from any other motive will learn no more in after life; some subjects he may continue to labour at from material considerations, but

> Farewell Horace whom I hated so.

Poetry taught for examination is like a little corn buried in a napkin where it can be dug up again for inspection. But if we regard school life as the seed-time for a harvest we ourselves shall never see, then we must consider how best to use the short, precious time so that the seed may bear fruit in after years. Only a very few hours weekly for a few years are available for poetry in school; but if we can, in that brief space, awaken a love for it, the child has a whole life-time in which to develop the subject, and, through it, his own being.

There is one good reason and only one for learning poetry—to increase our enjoyment of it.

I suggest, therefore, that in spite of tradition and inspectors and examinations we should give children a perfectly free option as to what poetry they should learn, and, failing to induce them to learn any, should not make a bad matter worse by forcing them to do so; and that in spite of superior persons, with their admirable maxim (for professors), 'aut professor aut nullus,' and their scorn of 'snippets', we should be content if our children learn the contents of their commonplace books, the short passages they have themselves selected for their bearing on their own lives and interests.

An acorn, fairly planted, may grow into a great tree, but a branch, however large, will wither if it is only stuck in.

The tree we want to raise is the love of fine poetry;

and from it, if we and our children are fortunate, another delightful shoot may spring: original verse.

The point I have been trying to make all through this essay is that poetry, its rhythm, its music, its imagery, its figures of speech, are instinctive in children, that they have a natural appetite for them, and an intuitive gift of using them. The reader will therefore not be surprised if I suggest that children can express themselves better in verse than in prose—I will not raise the question whether they *can* express themselves in prose.

I have found that some of the dullest boys, if given a suitable subject, tend naturally to write rhythmically, and instinctively resort to inversion in order to obtain rhythm; and verse is simply rhythm measured off in lines, so many stresses in each.

I lately recited Peacock's 'War Song' to some boys, and asked them to write an account of the raid, in the person either of a warrior who took part in it, or as a woman of the conquered tribe. One very primitive and usually very obtuse member of the class actually became for the time a savage and produced the following, written of course as prose, but I have marked off the rhythmic parts as verse.

> One morning when the sun was bright
> We gathered altogether.
> Five hundred strong were we
> And with our bows and glittering shields
> We marched off down to Dyfed.
> Ha! there we saw the cattle grazing
> And there our banner glittered,
> And then we gave a desperate rush
> And killed our foes in hundreds.

O'er many a dale our prizes went
And we marched just behind them.
We looked behind and there we saw both orphans
and widows;
They sobbed and sighed and bitterly cried,
But we marched off from Dyfed.

On the way we met their king so bold. He had with him two hundred bold men but not so bold as ours. He in his rage rushed at us but we stood strong together;

Eight score we slew and the rest they flew
But we marched on from Dyfed.

We sacked the gold and drank the wine and with our prizes we then marched home

On our way five score we met
But they flew in terror

My farm is now five hundred sheep
And as jolly was I never
In our house or hut we have both silver and gold.

It will be noticed that this has not only an unconscious rhythm and a feeling after rime but a well-marked tendency to repeat a burden or refrain. My cousin, Dr. William Lamborn, a Central African naturalist, tells me that he has observed exactly the same tendency in the 'chants' of primitive races, both in Africa and South America.

It is thus a complete mistake to regard original verse as an 'accomplishment' like the things taught in Miss Pinkerton's seminary: it is first of all a natural outlet for emotion; the child, like the true poet,

Sings because he must,
And pipes but as the linnet sings.

But it is incidentally also a very valuable training in choice of words and in literary style.

In a more advanced stage of scholarship that training is afforded by prose: we become our own critics, and will let no sentence stand till we have hunted through our vocabulary and found the words that most exactly express what we desire to say. But younger people have not the instinct for such nice discrimination. The exigencies of rime and rhythm, however, will compel them to examine their stock of words and to weigh their values for the desired purpose, to make sure of the exact meaning of many words which they know vaguely but would not otherwise use; such words thus become part of their actual, not merely of their potential, vocabulary. Equally valuable is the training in construction: if a statement will not 'beat' or rime in the form in which it first occurs to the mind, or, a still more important matter, if it does not *sound well* in the ear, they have to recast it until it assumes a suitable form. Such a process is of the very essence of good style.

In beginning class-teaching of original verse a well-marked rhythm is the first thing to aim at. Short riming couplets are perhaps the simplest form of approach. One couplet may be written on the blackboard, e. g.

> The snow is on the ground,
> It muffles every sound,

and the class should then *beat* the verse-rhythm

∪ – ∪ – ∪ –, ∪ – ∪ – ∪ –

on the desks or on their hands, repeating it several times till they have thoroughly got the *feel* of it.

Then suggestions for the beginning of another couplet

may be asked for; each boy who volunteers one should be required to beat it on the desk to prove its rhythm as he speaks it; the most popular line should then be written down; the class will readily see that they must choose one ending with a word that can be rimed, e. g.

Now all the air is hushed,

which might be suggested, would face them with the difficulty of getting a rime to 'hushed'. They may thus be led to express the same idea, either by inversion or by recasting, so as to end the line with a word that has more rimes, e. g.

Now hushed is all the air,

or,

The air is hushed and still.

Next, suggestions for the second line may be written down and criticized by the class as to smoothness of rhythm, exactness of rime, variety of vowel-sound, clearness and beauty of pictorial effect. For example, the line

And all the trees are still

may be offered to rime with 'still', and thus give an opportunity to distinguish between rime and assonance. Or,

The rill below the mill

will afford an example of the clash of rimes, jarring like neighbour notes, when they come too near together. Or,

A noise comes from the rill

will introduce, first, the objection to allowing stresses to fall on prepositions like 'from', and secondly, to the use of vague words like 'noise' instead of more precise or onomatopoetic words like music or murmur or babbling; so, perhaps, suggestion for an improved line may be offered, e.g.

I hear the murmuring rill.

Every opportunity should be taken to mark the distinction between a mere verse and a line of real poetry; that is, one with a fine picture or fine music in it.

After the couplet a quatrain of four lines with only two rimes, e.g. Mary's Lamb may be taken for a model and treated in the same way, and next a quatrain riming alternately, like the Casabianca stanza.

Only a little of this preliminary class work will be necessary. As soon as possible children should be allowed to attempt stanzas for themselves, choosing at first their own subject and metre; the class work should then be criticism of individual efforts. Two stanzas at least should be required in order to ensure that the unit chosen is properly repeated, e.g. a boy will perhaps produce one stanza riming *a b a b* and having four stresses to the line, and the next riming —*a* —*a* and having two lines of only three stresses. Children should be required at first to indicate the rimes and stresses at the end of each line *a* 4, *b* 3, *a* 4, *b* 3; so that they may themselves prove the uniformity of stanzas.

Later on, stanzas of set rime arrangements may be demanded, e.g.

a b a b c c

or *a a b a a b*

or *a b a b b a*

The last will lead up to the octave of the sonnet; and such stanzas as *a b c a b c*

or *a b b a b a*

will prepare for the sestet.

I repeat again that these things really present very little difficulty to boys: I lately asked inadvertently for a stanza riming

a a a b a a a b

really meaning

a a a b c c c b

and I was surprised to see how many boys succeeded in finding the necessary number of rimes.

The visible results of this kind of teaching will of course vary with the home advantages of the children: boys who often hear poetry quoted, and whose vocabulary is enriched, in conversation at home, will naturally produce better verse. For example, Mr. Caldwell Cook, who practised here when preparing for the Oxford Diploma in Education, has since, as the Persse Playbooks show, got much better poetry from the Persse schoolboys than he could get from our children; but that is not because any one social class has a monopoly of the poetic instinct, but because some children have less chance than others to develop it:

> Knowledge to their eyes her ample page,
> Rich with the spoils of time, did ne'er unroll;
> Chill penury repressed their noble rage,
> And froze the genial current of the soul.

But there cannot be a more unfortunate mistake than to measure the success of our teaching by its immediate results. To *write* poetically is natural and easy to children; but what we ought to desire for them is that they should think and *live* poetically as men. Their little exercises are but straws on the current. How they will make love at twenty, how they will use their leisure at thirty, what they will desire for their children at forty, what this life means to them at fifty and the next at seventy—these are ultimate and vital questions which the love of poetry will profoundly affect. And most of us can only hope to see the fruits of our labours with the eye of faith. Yet

> Others, I doubt not, if not we
> The issue of our toils shall see;
> And, they forgotten and unknown,
> Young children gather as their own
> The harvest that the dead have sown.

CHAPTER XI

AN ILLUSTRATIVE LESSON

'Here, now, is my way; where is thine? As for *the* way—it doth not exist.'

It may be useful if I give an account of a typical lesson; our study of Tennyson's 'Brook' may serve as the example.

Though few lessons, in literature at least, divide clearly into the five formal divisions of Herbartian psychologists, yet the five headings of that analysis may usefully be borne in mind; for a good teacher reviewing his lesson will usually find that, whether by instinct or design, most of the formal 'steps' are discoverable in its progress.

Thus he will begin with what the Herbartians call 'preparation', which may best be explained, perhaps, as winning the pupils' sympathies with what he is about to undertake. The 'preparation' for this particular lesson took place some days beforehand when the class was taken for a ramble along the course of Bayswater Brook, a small tributary of the Cherwell.

Nothing was said about the poem; but opportunity was made to speak of coots and herns when a water-hen was seen, to call a farmstead a thorp, to draw attention to eddies where the water swept round a little bay, to note the changes in the sound of the brook in different parts of its course, and to explain them by reference to the nature of its bed, to name the flowers growing in or near it, and, particularly, to point out the light-and-shade effect of the sunbeams shining through the overhanging foliage.

I was tempted, of course, all the time to quote from the poem itself, but I refrained in order that it might make its own appeal as a whole; and so I contented myself by drawing attention to the details that the poet would afterwards transfigure 'to make this much-loved earth more lovely'.

A few days afterwards, at school, I completed the preparation' stage by recalling the brook to memory, and telling the class that I was going to recite a poem which 'will show you the brook in such a way that when you see it again it will be different'.

Then came the 'presentation'. I recited the poem (with the book open at hand, for fear of accidents), trying both to make my rendering musical and also to make the music change alike with the changing motion of the stream and with the moods suggested by the poet's images.

The class meanwhile had their books open before them; and whether they looked at the words or at me, for they were free to do either, saw, I hope, the vision and the dream.

When I had finished I reminded the class that the poet's purpose had been to show them pictures and I inquired if any one's picture had been blurred by a word not understood. One or two explanations were asked for, but I had taken care, as an essential part of the preparation stage, that unfamiliar words like 'thorp' and 'shingly' should call up their appropriate images.

I next asked the class for comments upon anything that had struck them during my reading. The first suggestion was that 'the music agreed with the pictures'. I required illustrations and was given

> I chatter over stony ways
> I babble on the pebbles
> I chatter, chatter as I flow
> I murmur under moon and stars.

A second observation was that there were many contrasts in the poem; examples given were: between the ferny hollows of the hills and the flowery meadows of the lower course of the stream; between both the sound and the meaning in 'hurry' and in 'slip' and in 'chatter' and 'steal' and 'slide'; between the music and the motion of 'chatter over stony ways' and 'murmur under moon and stars'.

Thirdly it was pointed out that the repetition of the words 'Men may come and men may go, but I go on for ever' gave a sense of the age of the brook; which reminded another boy that the repetition of 'I' forced you to think of the brook as a living being. A further suggestion was made that there were many good epithets in the poem. I asked what a good epithet was and it was agreed that it was a word that makes you see the picture more clearly; examples offered were 'sudden', 'brimming', 'eddying', 'lusty', 'skimming', 'brambly'. Lastly a boy noted that many beautiful things were mentioned; and 'fairy foreland', 'blossom', 'sweet forget-me-nots', 'lovers', 'swallows', 'moon and stars', were given as instances.

No further comments being volunteered, I said I should

like to add something on some of the observations made but first to point out that nothing had been said of the colours in the pictures, no doubt because the words that give colour to them are not obviously 'coloured' terms. Nevertheless we are made to see the colours; for the lonely upland haunts of coot and hern are brown with dry rushes and heather and bare rock; and field and fallow together give a patchwork of shining grass and dark ploughland; wet pebbles shine like jewels in the sun; foam is white and gravel golden; there is light on the lawns and gloom under the hazel covers; there is morning sunshine, and night with her train of stars. . . .

Since the first truth about poetry is that the ear helps the eye to see I was most concerned to deepen the impression of a correspondence between the music and the images throughout the poem. I pointed out that this was effected not only by the use of sound-suggesting words like chatter and murmur but even more by words whose movement and rhythm corresponded to the motions described. 'Hurry' and 'slip' had already been mentioned and I showed how the effort required to sound the h and the r corresponded with the force in the turbulent water; while the ease with which the sibilant and liquid elements of 'slip' slipped off the tongue produced a contrast of effort as well as of image. In

> Out again, I curve and flow
> To join the brimming river

there was a sense of impeded force in the long vowels and staccato accents of the first line and of a free-running sweep in the short vowels of the second.

I went on, reaching here what I suppose the Herbartians

would call the 'association' stage, to illustrate by quotation from other poems. First, of course, from Shakespeare,

> The current that with gentle murmur glides,
> Thou know'st, being stopt, impatiently doth rage;
> But when his smooth course is not hindered
> He makes sweet music with th' enamelled stones,
> Giving a gentle kiss to every sedge
> He overtaketh in his pilgrimage.

Then, from the contrast between the music of the same stream in different parts of its course I went on to give examples of contrast between different rivers—between shallow Tweed and silent Till,

> Says Tweed to Till—
> 'Wha gars ye rin sae still?'
> Says Till to Tweed—
> 'Though ye rin swift indeed
> And I rin slaw,
> Whaur ye droon ae mon
> I droon twa',

and between Tennyson's brook and Denham's Thames—

> O, could I flow like thee, and make thy stream
> My great example, as it is my theme!
> Though deep, yet clear; though gentle, yet not dull;
> Strong without rage, without o'erflowing full.

There, after the sharps and trebles of the brook, is the deep bass of the brimming river. I emphasized my point by quoting from Longfellow's 'Rain in Summer', in which the roar and rush of the storm water is suggested in the force required to eject the g's and r's and t's as

It rushes along the roofs
Like the tramp of hoofs;
How it gushes and struggles out
From the throat of the overflowing spout!

and, in contrast, from the Poet Laureate's 'London Snow', full of hushing esses and p's and soft l's.

When men were all asleep the snow came flying
In large white flakes falling on the city brown,
Stealthily and perpetually settling and loosely lying,
Hushing the latest traffic of the drowsy town;
Deadening, muffling, stifling its murmurs failing,
Lazily and incessantly floating down and down:
Silently sifting and veiling road, roof and railing;
Hiding differences, making unevenness even,
Into angles and crevices softly drifting and sailing.

Similarly in referring to the effect of repetition I quoted Thomas Cromwell's last despairing letter to his merciless King, 'most gracious prince, I cry for mercy, mercy, mercy!' as an example of the way in which repetition moves and impresses us.

I reminded the children too that at the very point where we had crossed the brook by a modern bridge the Romans had carried their road across it by a paved ford: that from the hamlet by the ford that twelfth-century William de Stowford, who founded a hospital, still existing in their parish, had taken his name: that his lands in the valley of the brook belonged still to the Charity[1]: and that the name of the brook itself was said to be originally Bayards'-water, the watering-place of the war-horses.

The knights are dust, their good swords rust,

—but the brook goes on for ever.

[1] Now represented by Oriel College.

I reminded them, moreover, that repetition was a much more important element in the poem than had yet been noted. For the whole poem was built on a repetition of a regular pattern; first a line was made by unstressed and stressed syllables repeating alternately four times

·|·|·|·|

then a second line was added containing only three repetitions—so that change was combined with uniformity

·|·|·|·

next a stanza was built by repeating these lines alternately and making their end stresses also correspond alternately in sound ·|·|·|·|*a* ·|·|·|·*b* |·|·|·|*a* |·|·|·*b* and lastly by repetition of the stanza-pattern the whole poem was built up.

I explained that monotony was avoided by the varying force of the stresses—in

And sparkle out among the fern

the second and fourth stresses are stronger than either of the others and the first is stronger than the third, and also by the alternation throughout of masculine and feminine rimes, and, of course, by the introduction of fresh rimes in each new stanza.

I drew attention to the essential importance of preserving the conscious presence of a pattern in reading or reciting verse, and cautioned the class particularly of the danger in the rather difficult fifth stanza that the second rime should be lost through pausing at 'foreland' and running 'set' on to the next line: there must be a pause, distinct however short, on 'set' as well as on 'foreland'; yet, because the sense must be made clear no less than the pattern, there must be no dropping of the voice such as accompanies a pause in a prose reading.

So at the end of the seventh stanza there must be a pause to mark alike the rime and the end of the unit of pattern; but the sense 'runs on' and demands therefore that the voice be kept up.

I remarked upon the absence of figurative language in the poem, and pointed out that the single example had been overlooked, though it offered the best illustration of the poet's characteristic power of economizing language by concentrating meaning and pictorial effect in a single epithet: the metaphor 'netted' raised as by a charm a vision of the dappled surface of the brook as we had seen it when

> the sun came dazzling through the leaves.

Of the two remaining Herbartian stages 'application' would find its place in succeeding lessons when the class would comment on other poems in the light by which they had been helped to view this one, and still more, I hope, in the 'application' to any brook afterwards seen by the children of lines in the poem which seemed to them applicable.

Perhaps, too, the exercise I asked them to attempt, of writing an original stanza to be inserted in the poem at any suitable point, may be included under the head of 'application'.

Other exercises suggested were

1. Select the stanza you consider
    (*a*) the most musical
    (*b*) contains the most beautiful picture
    (*c*) contains the best example of the use of alliteration.

2. Find the lines nearest to the rhythm of Shakespeare's

> By what bypaths and indirect crooked ways.

and

> Swilled by the wild and wasteful ocean.

3. Most words are faded pictures : recover, by means of a good dictionary, the picture in 'cresses', 'loiter', and 'bicker'. N.B. A 'good' dictionary is one that explains the old as well as the modern uses of a word.

It will have been noted that there seems to be nothing in the lesson corresponding to the Herbartian 'formulation', no summing up in a sentence or two of 'the lesson the poem teaches us'.

The poem itself is the formulation. And, as Froude said of history, there are no lessons save in the emotions that arise in us as we read it.

It may be objected that to suggest preparation out of doors is to advocate a counsel of perfection.

If my subject had been Mr. Masefield's 'Posted as Missing' I should have been obliged to content myself by showing inland children who had never seen the sea a picture of a sailing ship, and pointing out her topsails and her port lantern before beginning my recitation. But the fact remains, and England will have to reckon with it, that no real education is possible, physical, mental, or spiritual, until the child is put into communion with Nature's handiwork as well as with man's.

I heard lately of a child who, taken for the first time into the country, came running to his Sunday School superintendent crying 'O teacher, there 's a sparrer up there and 'e cawnt git up and 'e cawnt git dahn—and 'e aint arf hollerin!'

> 'And singing still dost soar, and soaring ever singest.'

SUPPLEMENTARY EXERCISES

ILLUSTRATING CHAPTER X

SUPPLEMENT TO CHAPTER X

I GIVE as a supplement to this chapter a selection of verse exercises written by our children. And since examinations, however dangerous—like a burning-glass, in ignorant hands—do serve to bring aims as it were to a focus, I have added a selection of questions from examination papers which I have set in recent years and which I think must be unique, *because they have cost as much time and thought in the setting as is required in the answering*: when that is true of all examinations they will cease to be the curse and stumbling-block of education that now they are; they will then test, as these papers are designed to test, not mere brute memory but the higher, creative and critical, faculties of the mind; and call upon the pupils, and their teachers, to examine the basis of their tastes and opinions as opposed to their 'passions and prejudices masquerading as thoughts'.

The following types of Exercises are represented:

1.

Lines and stanzas to set patterns in which stressed syllables are represented by strokes, and unstressed by dots, and the rimes are indicated by letters: thus the pattern of a stanza of 'Mary's Lamb' would be shown as

| · | · | · |–
· | · | · | *a*
· | · | · | · |–
· | : | · :| *a*

2.

Stanzas on given models. Here the pupil has to discover and set out the pattern or rhythmic picture for himself before proceeding as in Ex. 1.

3.

Stanzas inserted into or added to poems. These must not merely correspond in form with those of the original but must fit into the picture, or continue the story.

4.

Bouts rimés: four or six words are given to be used as the rimes upon which a stanza is built.

5.

Old English Head-rimes on the model of 'Piers Plowman'.

6.

Free exercises in which the choice of form or subject, or of both, is left to the pupil.

In most of these exercises it will be noted that it is the form and not the subject that is set. Subject should be left to the child's own choice until he has achieved some considerable mastery over verse forms.

In my *Expression in Speech and Writing* (1922), I said that while I had never yet succeeded in getting boys to produce tolerable sonnets I still hoped to do so: some of the examples now given, I think, show that that hope has been realized.

Verses to a Set Pattern.

|·|·|·|·a In the trees the birds are singing,
|··|b For it is Spring;
|·|·|·|·a Through the woods the echoes ringing
|··|b Wake ev'rything;
|·|·|·|·c Men, the pretty birds are shooting,
|·|·|·|·c Naughty boys their eggs are looting,
|·|·|·|·c Owls begin their ghostly hooting—
|··|b They cannot sing.

|·|·|·|·a Pretty robins, also thrushes,
|··|b Are nesting here,
|·|·|·|·a All their nests are in the bushes
|··|b Each like a sphere;
|·|·|·|·c In the nest four eggs are lying,
|·|·|·|·c Here and there male birds are flying,
|·|·|·|·c Boys for robins' eggs are spying,
|··|b Robin is near.

|·|·|·|·a Soon the young ones will be hatching,
|··|b Male robins then
|·|·|·|·a Will be busy, much food catching,
|··|b All for the hen;
|·|·|·|·c She will to the young ones take it,
|·|·|·|·c They will eat it raw—not bake it
|·|·|·|·c They, I'm sure, will not forsake it—
|··|b They're happy then.

|·|·|·|·a Soon their nest they will be leaving,
|··|b Older are they,
|·|·|·|·a Up and down their wings they're heaving
|··|b All through the day.
|·|·|·|·c Up into the air they're flying,
|·|·|·|·c One is for his old nest sighing,
|·|·|·|·c Very soon he will be crying,
|··|b He wants to stay.

J. OSBORNE (9 yrs.).

Verses to a Set Pattern.

·|·|·|·|– The cuckoo comes to us in Spring,
·|·|·|*a* She sings her song so clear;
·|·|·|·|– And now the corncrake 's come to stay
·|·|·|*a* Which shows that Summer's near;
·|·|·|·|– Up in the tall and leafy elms
·|·|·|*a* The cries of rooks we hear.

·|·|·|·|– In fields along the country lanes
·|·|·|*a* The tall green grasses sway,
·|·|·|·|– Amongst them skylarks build their nests
·|·|·|*a* Of horses' hair and hay,
·|·|·|·|– While underneath the shady trees
·|·|·|*a* The sheep and cattle stay.

·|·|·|·|– The brook is sparkling in the sun,
·|·|·|*a* There is a gentle breeze,
·|·|·|·|– The little fish and wavelets dance
·|·|·|*a* Under the willow trees;
·|·|·|·|– Amongst the flowers upon the banks
·|·|·|*a* We hear the humming bees.

H. TUCKWELL (14 yrs.).

Verses to a Set Pattern.

MARSTON

·|·|·|·– The men that live at Marston,
·|·|·|*a* The wretched town of mud,
·|·|·|·– Migrate to better places,
·|·|·|*a* By swimming through the flood:
·|·|·|·– If any one could stop them,
·|·|·|*a* He very gladly would.

·|·|·|·– The savages from Marston,
·|·|·|*a* Are very fierce and strong,
·|·|·|·– They hunt the ancient mammoth,
·|·|·|*a* And stick him with a prong:
·|·|·|·– And then they sit a-feasting—
·|·|·|*a* And sing an ancient song.

·|·|·|·– Barbarians from Marston,
·|·|·|*a* Have dismal wretched caves,
·|·|·|·– And in them live the hunters,
·|·|·|*a* The women, and the braves,
·|·|·|·– And there they skin their mammoths—
·|·|·|*a* The poor, untidy knaves.

J. OSBORNE (10 yrs.).

Stanzas to Set Patterns in preparation for an attempt at Sonnet form.

·|·|·|·|·|*a* The clear and sparkling streams down hillsides flow,
·|·|·|·|·|*b* And over sand and pebbles make their way;
·|·|·|·|·|*b* Along their sides the bending reeds all sway,
·|·|·|·|·|*a* And wild forget-me-nots together grow.

·|·|·|·|·|*a* The chaffinch sings 'mid hawthorn bushes high,
·|·|·|·|·|*b* For finished is its lichen-covered nest,
·|·|·|·|·|*b* And in it soon some little eggs will rest
·|·|·|·|·|*a* From which there'll come young birds that cannot fly.

•|•|•|•|•|*a* On grassy hills the lambs all frisk and run
•|•|•|•|•|*b* For now has come the warm and flow'ry Spring;
•|•|•|•|•|*c* The grasses, trees, and hedges all are green
•|•|•|•|•|*a* For on them shines the bright, warm, golden sun;
•|•|•|•|•|*b* The nightingales their songs of joy now sing,
•|•|•|•|•|*c* But they are shy, and hardly ever seen.

ANDREW JAMES MARTIN (13 yrs.).

First Attempt at Sonnet Form.

•|•|•|•|•|*a* Now Summer's near, the birds and beasts are gay
•|•|•|•|•|*b* Because they know that hotter days draw nigh,
•|•|•|•|•|*b* The swift-winged martins dart across the sky,
•|•|•|•|•|*a* Or search for little bits of down and clay
•|•|•|•|•|*a* With which to build their nests before they lay;
•|•|•|•|•|*b* Up in the air the homeless cuckoos fly,
•|•|•|•|•|*b* And we may hear the joyous notes they cry;
•|•|•|•|•|*a* In pasture-lands the buttercups all sway,
•|•|•|•|•|*c* And look like one wide lake of shining gold,
•|•|•|•|•|*d* Among them many little lambs now run,
•|•|•|•|•|*e* While 'neath some green-clad trees are parent sheep
•|•|•|•|•|*e* That eat the tender grass, or go to sleep;
•|•|•|•|•|*d* Up in the heavens shines the golden sun,
•|•|•|•|•|*c* And banished are the Winter days so cold.

ANDREW JAMES MARTIN (13 yrs.).

Stanzas to Set Patterns in preparation for an attempt at Sonnet Form.

· | · | · | · | · | *a* I love to view the sparkling glassy pond,
· | · | · | · | · | *b* To see the graceful grasses bend and sway,
· | · | · | · | · | *b* And watch the merry snow-white lambs at play,
· | · | · | · | · | *a* And then to cast my weary eyes beyond,

· | · | · | · | · | *a* To see the starlings as for food they seek,
· | · | · | · | · | *b* And watch the rabbits as they race and run,
· | · | · | · | · | *b* I see the corn, that, ripened by the sun,
· | · | · | · | · | *a* Does bow and bend blown by the breezes bleak.

· | · | · | · | · | *a* I love to hear the blackbird as it sings,
· | · | · | · | · | *b* And sit within the shadows of the trees,
· | · | · | · | · | *c* Through which a golden sunbeam steals its way,
· | · | · | · | · | *a* And listen to the echo then that rings,
· | · | · | · | · | *b* Across the rocky hills and lovely leas,
· | · | · | · | · | *c* How glorious is the happy month of May!

BERNARD HAZELL (11 yrs.).

A First Attempt at Sonnet Form.

· | · | · | · | · | *a* The lovely flowers beside the wayside grow,
· | · | · | · | · | *b* The thrushes, in the bushes now do sing,
· | · | · | · | · | *b* Their happy voices welcome in the Spring,
· | · | · | · | · | *a* How lovely are they after all the snow,
· | · | · | · | · | *a* Soft breezes o'er the meadows green do blow,
· | · | · | · | · | *b* The sunbeams glitter like a proud young king,
· | · | · | · | · | *b* You see the tom-tit, on the bramble swing,

·|·|·|·|·|*a* The lovely roses, their full glory show,
·|·|·|·|·|*c* Soft showers of rain fall on the greening corn,
·|·|·|·|·|*d* Through which the rabbits race, and run, and play;
·|·|·|·|·|*c* How lovely is the world this spring-time morn!
·|·|·|·|·|*d* The trees, before the gentle breezes sway,
·|·|·|·|·|*c* The dark clouds by the sunlight bright are torn,
·|·|·|·|·|*d* It streams down on the golden, shining hay.

BERNARD HAZELL (11 yrs.).

Stanzas to Set Patterns in preparation for an attempt at Sonnet Form.

·|·|·|·|·|*a* The lark sings sweetly in the clear blue skies,
·|·|·|·|·|*b* And in the fields the flow'rs dance in the breeze;
·|·|·|·|·|*b* The cuckoo now sings gaily in the trees,
·|·|·|·|·|*a* And in the woods are heard wild pigeon's cries.

·|·|·|·|·|*c* The swifts and martins have come back at last,
·|·|·|·|·|*d* And now the thrushes sweetly sing all day,
·|·|·|·|·|*d* In the green fields the young lambs frisk and play,
·|·|·|·|·|*c* For Nature knows that Winter now is past.

·|·|·|·|·|*e* The dancing streamlets hurry down the hills,
·|·|·|·|·|*f* And now the sun shines brightly in the sky;
·|·|·|·|·|*g* The cows beneath the shady trees do rest,
·|·|·|·|·|*e* And rivers swiftly rush past ancient mills;
·|·|·|·|·|*f* The swallows gaily through the air do fly,
·|·|·|·|·|*g* And now the merry chaffinch sings its best.

ROBERT BAKER (13 yrs.).

First attempt at Sonnet Form.

JUNE

· | · | · | · | · | *a* The glorious month of June at last is here,
· | · | · | · | · | *b* And merry birds sing sweetly in the sky;
· | · | · | · | · | *b* The butterflies flit swiftly past on high,
· | · | · | · | · | *a* And now warm Summer days are drawing near;
· | · | · | · | · | *a* And over winding rivers bright and clear,
· | · | · | · | · | *b* The gaily coloured kingfisher doth fly;
· | · | · | · | · | *b* And in the woods is heard the jay's harsh cry;
· | · | · | · | · | *a* The finches' twitt'ring songs fill us with cheer.
· | · | · | · | · | *c* And in the fields the snow-white lambkins play,
· | · | · | · | · | *d* The cuckoos now sing gaily in the trees;
· | · | · | · | · | *e* The merry whitethroat now has built its nest,
· | · | · | · | · | *c* And in the fields the tall green grasses sway;
· | · | · | · | · | *d* The graceful flow'rs bend gently in the breeze,
· | · | · | · | · | *e* On elm tree tops the large black rooks do rest.

Robert Baker (13 yrs.).

First attempt at Sonnet Form.

· | · | · | · | · | *a* The dull and dreary clouds float o'er the sky,
· | · | · | · | · | *b* We do not hear the happy birds' sweet songs;
· | · | · | · | · | *b* Our merry friends have gone away in throngs,
· | · | · | · | · | *a* And all across the fields the wild flow'rs die,
· | · | · | · | · | *a* Their life has gone, and helplessly they lie,
· | · | · | · | · | *b* But they have died quite clean, they have no wrongs,
· | · | · | · | · | *b* And for their keen bright faces nature longs—
· | · | · | · | · | *a* The wind we hear is but her hopeless cry.

· | · | · | · | · | *c* The woodlands' weary hosts look almost dead,
· | · | · | · | · | *d* The trees sway in the wind, so rough and cold.
· | · | · | · | · | *e* The sun sends out a dull and feeble ray.
· | · | · | · | · | *c* The weeping willow its long leaves doth shed.
· | · | · | · | · | *d* The world which is so grey and worn and old,
· | · | · | · | · | *e* Still hopes that nature will be green some day.

FREDERICK NOEL EDGE (13 yrs.).

On the Model of 'In Memoriam'.

· | · | · | · | *a* The battle rages like a fire,
· | · | · | · | *b* The dreadful field is drowned in blood,
· | · | · | · | *b* Soldiers who fight in rain and mud
· | · | · | · | *a* Get caught like rats in the barbed wire.

FREDERICK NOEL EDGE (13 yrs.).

On the Model of Browning's 'Rabbi Ben Ezra'.

· | · | · | *a* The little birds are gay,
· | · | · | *a* And little lambs do play,
· | · | · | · | · | *b* The snowdrop bends its small white head so sweet,
· | · | · | *c* The sky is blue and clear,
· | · | · | *c* The dew lies like a tear,
· | · | · | · | · | · | *b* The thrush sings merrily and little lambs do bleat.
· | · | · | *a* The hedges are all green,
· | · | · | *a* The swallow can be seen,
· | · | · | · | · | *b* And April showers fall upon the ground,
· | · | · | *c* The daisies show their heads
· | · | · | *c* Above their grassy beds,
· | · | · | · | · | · | *b* And buds are coming out, and flowers grow around.

ERNEST BALL (13 yrs.).

On the Model of Browning's 'Rabbi Ben Ezra'.

·|·|·|*a* The merry Spring is here
·|·|·|*a* The flow'rs do now appear,
·|·|·|·|·|*b* And happy birds flit through the clear blue sky,
·|·|·|*c* All through the pleasant day
·|·|·|*c* Young lambs do frisk and play
·|·|·|·|·|·|*b* And in the air the blue-backed twitt'ring swallows fly.

·|·|·|*a* The birds have flown away
·|·|·|*a* To bright lands warm and gay,
·|·|·|·|·|*b* For now the dark and dreary days are near;
·|·|·|*c* The bulbs are tucked in bed,
·|·|·|*c* Leaves on the ground are dead,
·|·|·|·|·|·|*b* And now the cold and dreaded Winter winds are here.

ROBERT BAKER (13 yrs.).

On the Model of Swinburne's 'Garden of Proserpine'.

·|·|·|·*a* The snow is gently falling
·|·|·|*b* The clouds are dull and grey.
·|·|·|·*a* And robins are all calling,
·|·|·|*b* The little children play.
·|·|·|·*c* And all church-bells are ringing,
·|·|·|·*c* Melodious choirs are singing,
·|·|·|·*c* The mill his arms is flinging,
·|·|·|*b* So freely all the day.

FREDERICK NOEL EDGE (13 yrs.).

On the Model of Swinburne's 'Baudelaire'.

•|•|•|•|•|•a Beside the stream the willow trees are swaying
•|•|•|•|•|b While in the cooling shade the cattle sleep
•|•|•|•|•|b And on the grassy slopes are lazy sheep,
•|•|•|•|•|•a Young lambs that never seem to tire are playing
•|•|•|•|•|c And birds that fly about with joy do sing
•|•|•|•|•|c For they all know that now has come the Spring.
•|•|•|•|•|d Wild flowers are blooming 'neath the woodland trees,
•|•|•|•|•|e The rabbits frisk about and have much fun,
•|•|•|•|•|d While overhead are humming busy bees
•|•|•|e All brought out by the sun.

ANDREW JAMES MARTIN (13 yrs.).

On the Model of Swinburne's 'Baudelaire'.

•|•|•|•|•|•a The weary Winter 's past, and Spring is coming,
•|•|•|•|•|b The birds begin to sing up in the trees,
•|•|•|•|•|b The wind has fallen to a gentle breeze
•|•|•|•|•|•a And happy working bees now start their humming,
•|•|•|•|•|c And in the fields are flowers; while all the day
•|•|•|•|•|c Are jolly, little, new-born lambs at play,
•|•|•|•|•|d And busy streamlets hurry down the hills
•|•|•|•|•|e And just like gold, they sparkle in the sun.
•|•|•|•|•|d They trickle in between the daffodils;
•|•|•|e And there they play and run.

FREDERICK NOEL EDGE (13 yrs.).

On the Model of Matthew Arnold's 'Scholar Gipsy'.

·|·|·|·|·|*a* The birds are singing on the swaying trees,
·|·|·|·|·|*b* Their songs are bubbling o'er with Summer mirth,
·|·|·|·|·|*c* And mother birds their young do fondly scold
·|·|·|·|·|*b* If they attempt to fly down to the earth;
·|·|·|·|·|*c* In fields are daisies with their hearts of gold
·|·|·|*a* All dancing in the breeze.
·|·|·|·|·|*d* The corn is rip'ning in the Summer sun
·|·|·|·|·|*e* But in the harvest it will all be cut,
·|·|·|·|·*e* The lark when startled flies up from a rut,
·|·|·|·|·|*d* And little rabbits through the cornfields run.

Andrew James Martin (13 yrs.).

On the Model of Mr. Robert Bridges' 'Elegy on a Young Lady'.

THE FOX HUNT

|·|·|·|·|*a* It is a Winter day, the sun shines bright,
·|·|·|·|·|*b* The hounds do meet for there's to be a chase,
·|·|·|·|·|*a* The hunters in their red coats are a sight,
·|·|·|·|·|*b* The hounds are eager to start off the race,
·|·|·|*b* They're hard to keep in place.
·|·|·|·|·*c* And now the pack moves off with baying,
·|·|·|·|·|*a* From out the woods a vixen takes to flight,
·|·|·|·|·|·*c* And as the horses run they stop their neighing.

Robert Owens (10 yrs.).

On the Model: ' Thou that madest Earth and Heaven '.

|·|·|·|·*a* Flowers in the fields are bending
|··|*b* Their pretty heads,
|·|·|·|·*a* Sparkling streams their ways are wending
|··|*b* Through rocky beds;
|·|·|·|·*c* Now we hear the cuckoos singing,
|·|·|·|·*c* Cowslip bells have started ringing,
|·|·|·|·*c* Everywhere the flowers are springing;
|··|*b* Yellows and reds.

|·|·|·|·*a* O, the Winter winds are over,
|··|*b* Now it is Spring,
|·|·|·|·*a* Cattle feed among the clover,
|··|*b* Birds sweetly sing;
|·|·|·|·*c* Larks high up in air are flying,
|·|·|·|·*c* Plovers in the fields are crying,
|·|·|·|·*c* In the folds young lambs are lying,
|··|*b* It is the Spring.

R. BAKER (14 yrs.).

A Stanza added to Peacock's ' War Song '.

·|·|·|·*a* Into the peaceful valley
·|·|·|·*b* O'er rocks the thieves come leaping,
·|·|·|·*a* And made a sudden sally
·|·|·|·*b* On homes where men were sleeping,
·|·|·|·*c* There was an awful slaying
·|·|·|·*d* And fiercely raged the battle,
·|·|·|·*c* The widowed wives were praying
·|·|·|·*d* While thieves stole sheep and cattle.

ANDREW JAMES MARTIN (13 yrs.).

Original Stanzas added to.

·|·|·|·|·|·|·|·| *a* 'The honeysuckle round the porch has woven its wavy bowers,
·|·|·|·|·|·|·|·| *a* And in the meadow trenches blow the faint, sweet cuckoo flowers.'

·|·|·|·|·|·|·|·| *a* The daisies and the buttercups sway gently in the breeze,
·|·|·|·|·|·|·|·| *a* The farmer could not plough his field, but now he does with ease.

·|·|·|·|·|·|·|·| *a* He toils so hard to sow his seed, and then goes home to rest,
·|·|·|·|·|·|·|·| *a* The birds they take the seeds and then they go back to the nest.

·|·|·|·|·|·|·|·| *a* The birds are sitting on their eggs, the season now is Spring,
·|·|·|·|·|·|·|·| *a* And while they're sitting on their eggs the swallow 's on its wing.

·|·|·|·|·|·|·|·| *a* The petals of the roses drop upon the garden wall,
·|·|·|·|·|·|·|·| *a* And then the merry blackbird chirps and gives the birds a call.

·|·|·|·|·|·|·|·| *a* The butterflies flit round the yellow catkins, Spring is here,
·|·|·|·|·|·|·|·| *a* The wind that howls, the showers in May, the birdies do not fear.

SYDNEY JOHN CASTLE (9 yrs.).

Stanza with given Rhymes.

viz : eyes, shies, tell, well, done, run.

·|·|·|·| *a* The little birds are sleeping well
·|·|·| *b* The day of toil is done
·|·|·|·| *c* The tawny owls flit 'neath the skies

·|·|·|*a* Their hoots and screeches tell
·|·|·|·|*b* The rats the mice and voles to run
·|·|·|*c* Far from their searching eyes.

H. TUCKWELL (14 yrs.).

A Stanza written with given Rhymes.
viz.: skies, run, well, tell, done, eyes.

·|·|·|·|*a* The birds are flying in the skies,
·|·|·|·|*b* And in the meadow horses run,
·|·|·|·|*c* The country folk are by the well,
·|·|·|·|*c* And they all have a tale to tell,
·|·|·|·|*b* At last their merry tales are done,
·|·|·|·|*a* They go to bed and close their eyes.

JAMES ERIC MAYCOCK (9 yrs.).

A Stanza written with given Rhymes.
viz.: eyes, tell, run, skies, well, done.

·|·|·|·|*a* The little flow'rs now close their eyes,
·|·|·|*b* How soon the day is done.
·|·|·|·|*a* All red with sunset are the skies,
·|·|·|*b* The lambs no longer run.
·|·|·|·|*c* And by their bleating one can tell,
·|·|·|*c* That all with them is well.

LIONEL ABBOTT (10 yrs.).

Parody on 'Home Thoughts from Abroad'.

Oh to be in England
Now that Spring's begun,
And whoever wakes up early,
Has some jolly, merry fun;
In the lowest boughs the old jackdaw chats,
'Mongst the tiny leaves fly the teasing gnats,
While the cat 'sings' tunes on the orchard bough
In England—now.

S. CASTLE (10 yrs.).

Old English Head Rhymes.

OUR WALK

The weather was warm when we went for our walk,
And the boys with them brought all their bags packed with food,
Many fields were with flowers and grasses all filled,
And a rabbit once rapidly ran through the grass
When startled from sleeping by some one near by.
'Neath some trees we retired and then took out our food,
And we fed till we felt quite refreshed and much strengthened,
For we were weary of wandering through wilds and through fields.
When we'd finished our food, we all fled to a pit,
Where we slid down the slopes and climbed up the sides,
We went through a wood on our way towards home
And some bluebells were blown by a gentle, cool breeze.
At a brook thirsty boys filled some bottles with water,
To drink when they were dry and felt like dropping,
The swift-flying swallows went swooping o'er the Thames,
To find some fat flies on which they could feed,
When we finished at the ferry we felt very tired,
For we'd taken a tramp about ten miles long.

ANDREW MARTIN (13 yrs.).

Free choice of Form and Subject.

FROM MY WINDOW

·|·|·|·|– Oh from my window I can see,
·|·|·|*a* The rose of pretty hue,
·|·|·|·|– And trim white yachts do skim about,
·|·|·|*a* Across the ocean blue.

·|·|·|·|– The merry little children play
·|·|·|*a* Upon the golden sand,
·|·|·|·|– And from the pier sweet music comes,
·|·|·|*a* It is the Folkestone band.

·|·|·|·|– The slender trees dance in the sun,
·|·|·|*a* Through them the swallows fly,
·|·|·|·|– It fills the whole world with delight,
·|·|·|*a* When larks sing in the sky.

·|·|·|·|– Old seamen sitting in their boats,
·|·|·|*a* Take people out to sea,
·|·|·|·|– They do not take them very far
·|·|·|*a* But soon collect their fee.

·|·|·|·|– And sometimes little fishing smacks,
·|·|·|*a* Go out to sea at night,
·|·|·|·|– And in the morning they return,
·|·|·|*a* With herrings fresh and bright.

·|·|·|·|– And old men sitting in deck-chairs,
·|·|·|*a* Read papers all the day,
·|·|·|·|– They get so cross when children small,
·|·|·|*a* Around them start to play.

R. Baker (14 yrs.).

Original verses.. My own choice of Form.

APRIL

·|· · ·|*a* Which month brings us the fresh'ning show'rs?
·|·|·|·|*b* Who makes the grass shoot on the hill?
·|·|·|·|*a* Who brings us now the pretty flow'rs?
·|·|·|*b* 'Tis you, 'Tis you, April.

·|·|·|·|*a* Who makes the birds build in the trees?
·|·|·|·|*b* Who makes the moss grow by the rill?
·|·|·|·|*a* Who owns of Spring the charming keys?
·|·|·|*b* 'Tis you, 'Tis you, April.

·|·|·|·|*a* Who brings the yellow buttercup?
·|·|·|·|*b* And the primrose and the daffodil?
·|·|·|·|*a* Who makes the buds of trees shoot up?
·|·|·|*b* 'Tis you, 'Tis you, April.

·|·|·|·|*a* April, you bring us joy and sun,
·|·|·|·|*b* You brighten up our land with flow'rs,
·|·|·|·|*a* You make the hare begin to run,
·|·|·|*b* And O, those helpful show'rs.

PHILIP EDMONDS (10 yrs.).

Free choice of Form.

MAY

|··|*a* Sunshine at last
|··|*a* Showers are past
·|·|*b* The spring flowers sway
·|·|*b* This happy May.

·|··|*a* And all the birds sing
·|·|*a* The woodlands ring
|··|*b* Green are the trees,
|··|*b* There is a breeze.

|··|*a* And in the morn,
·|·|*a* The young green corn
|··|*b* Sways in the sun
·|·|*b* The field-mice run.

| · | *a*   By the stream
· | · | *a*   The sunbeams gleam
| · · | *b*   Primroses fade
· · | · | *b*   In the forest shade.

FREDERICK NOEL EDGE (13 yrs.).

Free choice of Form and Subject.

CALLERS AT THE DOOR

'Ah' said ma, with a hand to her head,
'Now at last I can rest in bed,
I've never worked so hard before',
But a sudden rat-tat at the door
Prevented ma from saying more.
Rat-tat-tat! there 'tis again!
Above the swishing of the rain.
Poor Mrs. Simpson hurried once more
Out of the room—and found at the door
A boy; his coat-collar was turned up,
He held in his arms a whining pup.
'Please buy this dog that I 'ave 'ere,
It's only a shilling—not very dear.'
'No thank you', Mrs. Simpson said,
And then she hurried off to bed.

But a knock came quickly, again and again,
The milkman stood in the driving rain;
Cried he 'There's 10*s*. 6*d*. to pay—
Please hurry I can't wait all day.'
But Mrs. Simpson only sighed,
'You'll have to wait a bit,' she cried.
'The baker's cart is drawing near,
And I have much to pay I fear.

I cannot pay you all I owe
You'll have to wait awhile you know.'
'I cannot wait', the milkman cried,
'Oh dear', unlucky mother sighed.
'I've got to buy some food to eat,
You really must wait till next week.'
'Very well then', grumbled the man
'You'll have to pay me all you can'.

The baker stept into the road,
And looked to see what mother owed.
'You owe me 4*s*. 10*d*.' he cried
But Mrs. Simpson only sighed.
'All right, I'll soon pay up', she said.
'And then, perhaps, I'll go to bed.'
The milkman and the bak'r are gone
And Mrs. Simpson's work is done,
And so with feet as heavy as lead
She drags herself upstairs to bed.

J. OSBORNE (10 yrs.).

ORIGINAL LIMERICKS

·· | ·· | ·· | *a* There was once a young lady of Clyde,
·· | ·· | ·· | *a* Who fell off her cycle and died,
·· | ·· | *b* She is now in a box,
·· | ·· | *b* In her Sunday-best socks;
·· | ·· | ·· | *a* And she's had, in the hearse, a good ride.

·· | ·· | ·· | *a* There is an old fellow called Gramp,
·· | ·· | ·· | *a* He's a wicked and artful old scamp,
·· | ·· | *b* Yet the silly old fool,
·· | ·· | *b* Comes and sits in our school—
·· | ·· | ·· | *a* Comes to school at the age of a Gramp!

··|··|··|*a* In our class there 's a fellow named Green,
··|··|··|*a* A worse fellow I never have seen,
··|··|*b* He has hair which is white,
··|··|*b* It 's a terrible sight;
··|··|··|*a* He has got the right name for he 's—green.

S. CASTLE (10 yrs.).

QUESTIONS

1. Instead of saying 'At Daybreak' Tennyson says

> When merry milkmaids click the latch,
> And rarely smells the new-mown hay,
> And the cock has sung beneath the thatch
> Twice or thrice his roundelay.

Try to *write* something of the kind, not necessarily in verse, for 'At Evening', and *quote* a passage that similarly speaks of Place instead of Time.

2. Rewrite the following passages in verse, giving in each instance a plan (*a*) of the rimes, (*b*) of the beats:

'Now who shall arbitrate? Ten men love what I hate, shun what I follow, slight what I receive; ten who in ears and eyes match me: we all surmise—they, this thing and I, that. Whom shall my soul believe?'

'In one year they sent a million fighters forth, south and north, and they raised their gods a brazen pillar, high as the sky; yet reserved a thousand chariots in full force—gold of course.'

3. Say what you can about the metaphor which calls the birch 'The Lady of the Woods'; and then find metaphors to describe its catkins and its bark.

4. Quote three passages you know to illustrate (*a*) Sound echoing sense, (*b*) Colour in words, (*c*) Musical speech.

5. In what order of preference would you place the following passages?[1] Give your reasons in the case of the passages you place first and last.

[1] Stanzas from 'Thyrsis', 'Mariamne', 'The Tiger', 'Three Years She Grew', and four of doggerel or bombast invented for the purpose of the question.

6. Mention any place you know which a poet might have had in mind in writing any passage you can quote. Give your reasons for thinking so.

7. Which of the following do you think might be improved by re-writing?[1] Try your hand on what you consider the worst of them.

8. 'Home, Rose and Home, Provence and La Palie.' Can you tell from this fragment whether or not it is a part of poetry?

9. Use 'sword' 'child' and 'dead' as metaphors, and 'down' and 'daffodil' in similes.

10. Tell the story of Alfred and the Cakes in the present tense *or* in the first person.

11. Taking the first stanza of 'After Blenheim' as an example, write a short prose picture of A Time and Place. (When this had been done the boys were asked to review their scenes and rewrite them so as (*a*) to make the picture clearer, (*b*) to introduce living things, movement, or colour, (*c*) to improve the sound of their exercise.)

12. Give an example of poetry in prose, and one of verse that is not poetry, and state briefly your reasons in each case.

13. Clomb above the eastern bar
The hornèd Moon, with one bright star
Within the nether tip.

Coleridge knew as well as every schoolboy that this phenomenon is impossible in nature. Can you justify his disregard of astronomical fact in this poem?

[1] A scene from 'Robinson Crusoe', a stanza of Adelaide Procter, a vague Latinized passage from a School History, and a stanza of 'The Forsaken Merman'.

14. Write a short address to a Star or a Stream as to a Person.

15. Say what pleased you in any poem you have heard or read so often as to know it fairly well.

16. Describe the print shown you (Elmer Keene's 'Wild Waters') as if you could see the colours of the original.

17. Sir Philip Sidney said that the function of poetry was 'to make this much loved earth more lovely'; quote not more than four passages that might be used to illustrate this.

18. What do you understand by a fine epithet? Illustrate by examples.

19. Mention any poems or prose passages that would help you in writing a description of a Ship, a Sunset, April, and a Mother's Love; and give one quotation in each instance.

20. What marks of poetry do you find in the following passages (Ruth i. 16–18; 2 Sam. xviii. 33; Job xxviii. 5–8)?

21. The cock's shrill clarion, or the echoing horn,
No more shall rouse them from their lowly bed.

Why is 'clarion' a metaphor and 'bed' not one?

22. Using Nathan's message to David as an example write a parable or allegory to give a picture of Germany's treatment of Belgium *or* of the position of the United States with regard to the war.

23. Complete, according to your own ideas, the picture (*or* the story) begun in the following stanza[1], in others of the same form.

[1] Stanzas invented for the purposes of the question, of a more or less difficult form according to the capacity of the class.

PRINTED IN ENGLAND AT THE OXFORD UNIVERSITY PRESS
BY JOHN JOHNSON PRINTER TO THE UNIVERSITY

Some Oxford Books on ENGLISH

¶ *General.*

THE TEACHING OF ENGLISH, by W. S. TOMKINSON. Pp. 230. 4s. 6d. net.

'It is full of good things.' *Educational Times.*

THE RUDIMENTS OF CRITICISM, by E. A. G. LAMBORN. Pp. 192. 3s. 6d. net.

POETIC VALUES, by E. A. G. LAMBORN. A Guide to the appreciation of *The Golden Treasury.* Pp. 238. 3s. 6d. net.

EXPRESSION IN SPEECH AND WRITING, by E. A. G. LAMBORN. Pp. 120. 3s. 6d. net.

'It is hard to over-praise this inspiring little book, written with all the author's raciness, humour, and enthusiasm. It deals in five chapters with oral and written composition, verse-making, original music, and the rendering of poetry.' *A. M. A.*

¶ *Phonetics.*

THE SOUNDS OF ENGLISH, by HENRY SWEET. Pp. 140. 3s. 6d. n.

An elementary introduction to Phonetics with particular reference to Standard English.

A PRIMER OF SPOKEN ENGLISH. Introduction, Analysis, Synthesis, by HENRY SWEET. 4th edition revised. 1911. Pp. 110. 3s. 6d. net.

PHONETIC TRANSCRIPTIONS OF ENGLISH PROSE, by DANIEL JONES. Pp. 60. 2s. 6d. net.

EXAMINATION PAPERS IN PHONETICS, by DANIEL JONES. Pp. 52. 2s. 6d. net.

Designed to furnish practice for Oxford, Cambridge, and London Certificates.

¶ *English Grammar, Descriptive.*

THE GATEWAY TO ENGLISH, by H. A. TREBLE and G. H. VALLINS.

I. First Steps in Grammar and Expression. Pp. 112. 2*s.* II. Grammar and the Simple Essay. Pp. 140. 2*s.* 6*d.* III. The Essentials of Formal Composition. Pp. 123. 2*s.* 6*d.* IV. Style in Composition. Pp. 231. 3*s.* 6*d.*

ELEMENTARY LESSONS IN ENGLISH GRAMMAR, by H. C. WYLD. Pp. 224. 2*s.* 6*d.*

A NEW ENGLISH GRAMMAR based on the recommendations of the Joint Committee on Grammatical Terminology by E. A. SONNENSCHEIN, with exercises by E. ARCHIBALD. Part I, 1s. 6d.; Part II, 2s.; Part III, 2s. 6d. Also in one volume, pp. 426. 5s.

SENTENCE ANALYSIS for the lower forms of Public Schools, by H. W. FOWLER. Pp. 68. 2s.

'A clear, simple, and exact practical exposition of the subject, produced in typographical form which leaves nothing to be desired.' *Pitman's Journal.*

For books marked with a dagger, thus †, teachers' Keys are available. Prices and conditions may be had on application to the publisher.

March 1929

Some Oxford Books on English

¶ English Historical Grammar.

A PRIMER OF HISTORICAL ENGLISH GRAMMAR, by HENRY SWEET. Second edition. Pp. 120. 3s.

A SHORT HISTORICAL ENGLISH GRAMMAR, by HENRY SWEET. Corrected impression. 1924. Pp. 276. 4s. 6d. net.

NEW ENGLISH GRAMMAR: Logical and Historical, in two parts, by HENRY SWEET.

Part I: Introduction, Phonology, and Accidence. Pp. 524. 10s. 6d. n. Part II: Syntax. Pp. 148. 5s. net.

A PRIMER OF ENGLISH ETYMOLOGY, by W. W. SKEAT. Sixth edition, revised. 1923. Pp. 120. 2s. 6d. net.

Chapters on the Sources of the Language; the History, Symbols and Sounds; Modern English Spelling; Words of Native Origin; Vowel Mutation and Gradation, &c.

STANDARD ENGLISH, by T. NICKLIN. (World's Manuals, No. 23.) Pp. 102. 2s. 6d. net.

'The author pleads that all children of whatever birth shall be carefully taught the "standard dialect"—the English, that is to say, of the educated class, and often hitherto regarded as a prerogative of that class.' *Journal of Education.*

ON THE RELATIONS BETWEEN SPOKEN AND WRITTEN LANGUAGE, by HENRY BRADLEY. Pp. 36. 2s. net.

An examination of the difficulties of spelling reform.

¶ Dictionaries.

A DICTIONARY OF MODERN ENGLISH USAGE, by H. W. FOWLER. Pp. 750. 7s. 6d. net. On India paper, 10s. net.

This book might be described as *The King's English* converted into a dictionary, but it contains more matter than the earlier work.

¶ THE POCKET OXFORD DICTIONARY OF CURRENT ENGLISH, compiled by H. W. and F. G. FOWLER. Pp. 1016. Cloth, 3s. 6d. net. India paper, 6s. net.

An authoritative guide to the latest and best English usage. Over 2,000 columns of clear type; yet the volume is small enough to be carried in the pocket of a traveller or holiday-maker.

¶ THE CONCISE OXFORD DICTIONARY, compiled by H. W. and F. G. FOWLER. Second Edition, 1929. Pp. 1460. From 7s. 6d. net.

¶ The *Pocket Oxford Dictionary* and the *Concise Oxford Dictionary* are of unrivalled authority because they alone among one-volume dictionaries are based on the great OXFORD ENGLISH DICTIONARY, edited by the late Sir James Murray, the late Dr. Bradley, Sir William Craigie, and Dr. Onions. Of this great work Vol. I was published in 1888 after many years of preparation; vol. X (the last) is now published. The complete work contains articles on about 425,000 words and extends to over 15,000 large pages, each of three columns. For details see the General Catalogue.

A CONCISE ETYMOLOGICAL DICTIONARY, by W. W. SKEAT; new and corrected impression. 1911. Pp. 680. 6s. net; on thin paper, 7s. 6d. net.

CAMPION
COLLEGE
A M
D G